the book of
babies' names

First published by Parragon in 2009

Parragon
Queen Street House
4 Queen Street
Bath BA1 1HE, UK

ISBN: 978-1-4075-4353-6

Written by Noam Friedlander
Internals designed by Talking Design
Created and produced by Design Principals.
Cover image: Infant baby © Getty Images.

Printed in China

the book of
babies' names

Parragon

Bath · New York · Singapore · Hong Kong · Cologne · Delhi · Melbourne

introduction

Choosing a name for your child is probably one of the most important things you will ever do for him or her. A name can be a reflection of character and identity and is an important first impression by which people are judged. When you look through this book to choose a name, bear in mind the following hints and suggestions. Good luck!

Some parents like to choose names that have important or meaningful associations—whether they are places, emotions, or family names. You might want to choose a name that reminds you of something significant. You can name your child after a family member, whether dead or alive, though remember that some religious cultures consider it bad luck to name a child after a living member of the family. To avoid this, you can always change the name slightly or choose an alternative version of it.

There are no rules that say you have to pick a name from your own ethnic background. However, some people think that taking a name from your own particular heritage can offer a source of identity to your child.

Some people worry about choosing names that do not clearly define their child's gender, while others consider it less important. There are many names that are popular for both girls and boys, so obviously if you have a problem with ambiguous names, then these should be the first names off your list.

Some parents go for unusual names to avoid the problem of their child having the same name as many others. Some names have many variations and spelling options, which may help to strike a balance and find a name that is distinctive and exclusive but isn't too unusual or odd.

There are advantages and disadvantages to having an ordinary or a unique name. While the common names might be easier to spell or pronounce, an unusual name might make your child stand out and feel special. Just because some names cause difficulties due to people's unfamiliarity with them, it doesn't mean you should avoid choosing them.

Be careful to make sure your child's initials don't spell or represent anything undesirable, especially when you include the middle names.

For some people it is important to choose a name with an upbeat meaning, because this positive meaning will be associated with your child. You can choose names that refer to qualities or traits that you hope your child will have, names with meanings that have special significance for you, or names that describe physical qualities that might be obvious in your baby.

Make sure your child's first name doesn't sound foolish when added to your surname. For example, someone with the last name Berry should probably not be called Logan and someone with the last name Walker should possibly not be given the name Luke, especially with the middle name Sky! If you have a common surname, such as Smith or Jones, an exciting or unusual name can spice it up a bit. For example, John Smith or Anne Jones could become Jaden Smith or Destiny Jones.

Before picking that special name, think about ways it can be shortened. Some nicknames may sound foolish alongside the child's surname. Some examples would be Barbara Dwyer (Barb Dwyer), Sylvester Fox (Sly Fox), and William Power (Will Power). Your child could insist on using their formal name, rather than the nickname, but this might not always be possible, especially if they're being teased in class or by their work colleagues.

You may want to pick a name that has a lot of nicknames and variations, such as Elizabeth or John, so that your child will have more control over his or her name when they're older. The only danger in doing this is that a childhood nickname may stick through adult life and could sound foolish.

Some names never drop out of the most popular names lists—names such as Jack and Thomas or Sarah and Emma. However, names do tend to follow trends or cycles of popularity and are often influenced by popular figures of the time. Back in the 1930s the name Shirley dominated top ten lists due to the popularity of Shirley Temple. Later Ryan, for Ryan O'Neal and even Demi, after Demi Moore, appeared in the top 100 list back in 1994.

When choosing your child's name, try to be objective and sure that the name will sound just as good in fifty years or so. Your child may not appreciate being named after pop or TV icons from the "ancient" past.

Before finalizing your child's name, it is a good idea to talk to your friends and family to ask their opinion. Not everyone will agree with your choice but they might provide some welcome help.

Boys' Names

A

Aaron:
From the Hebrew meaning "exalted," "enlightened." *Alternative spellings:* Aaran, Aarao, Aharon, Aranne, Arek, Aren, Arin, Aron, Aronek, Aronne, Aronos, Haroun, Harun. *Short forms:* Ari, Arni, Ron, Ronnie, Ronny.

Abdullah:
From the Arabic meaning "servant of Allah." *Alternative spellings:* Abdalla, Abdulla. *Short forms:* Abdal, Abdul, Del.

Abel:
From the Hebrew meaning "vanity" or "breath" or the Assyrian meaning "son." *Short forms:* Abe, Abie.

Abraham:
From the Hebrew meaning "father of many." *Alternative spellings:* Abrahamo, Abrahan, Abrahim, Abram, Avraham, Avram, Avrum, Ibrahim. *Short forms:* Ab, Abe, Abi, Bram.

Ace:
From the Latin *as,* meaning "unity."

Adam:
From the Hebrew *adamah,* meaning "red earth" or "from the earth." *Alternative spellings:* Ad, Adamec, Adamek, Adan, Adao, Adas, Addis, Addy, Ade, Adem.

Adan:
The Spanish form of Adam.

Addison:
From Old English meaning "Adam's son."

Aden:
See Aiden.

Adin:
From the Hebrew meaning "pleasure given" or the Old Norse meaning "delicate."

Adir:
From the Hebrew meaning "majestic" or "noble."

Aditya:
From the Sanskrit meaning "the sun."

Adolfo:
The Spanish form of Adolph.

Adolph:
From the Old German meaning "noble" or "wolf." *Alternative spellings:* Adolf, Adolphus. *Short forms:* Dolph, Dolphus.

Adonis:
From the Phoenician meaning "lord."

A

Adrian:

From the Latin meaning "man from Adria" (the Adriatic Sea region). *Alternative spellings:* Adriano, Adrien, Adrik, Adrion, Adron, Hadrian.

Adriel:

From the Hebrew meaning "of God's flock" or "God's majesty." *Alternative spellings:* Adri, Adrial. *Short form:* Ari.

Aedan:

See Aidan.

Agustin:

See Augustine.

Ahab:

From the Hebrew meaning "father's brother."

Ahmed:

From the Arabic meaning "much praised." *Alternative spellings:* Ahmad, Amad, Amadi.

Aiden:

From the Gaelic meaning "fire" or "little fiery one" or the Latin *adjuvare,* meaning "to help," via the Middle English *eyeden* and *aiden*. *Alternative spellings:* Aden, Aidan, Aidyn, Edan, Eden.

Ainsley:

From the Scottish meaning "own place" or "my field." *Alternative spellings:* Anslee, Ansley, Anslie, Ansy.

Ajay:

From the Sanskrit meaning "invincible" or the Punjabi meaning "victorious."

Al:

Short form of names beginning Al-.

Alan:

The origin of this name is disputed, possibly from the Gaelic meaning "fair," "handsome," "bright"; the Welsh meaning "harmony," "peace"; or the Irish meaning "noble." *Alternative spellings:* Alain, Allan, Allen, Alun.

Alard:

From the shortened version of the Old German name Athal, meaning "noble," and *hardu* meaning "hard," "tough and resilient" or "noble."

Alasdair:

The Gaelic form of the Greek name Alexander, meaning "defender of men." *Alternative spellings:* Alastair, Aldair, Alistair, Alister, Allister. *Short forms:* Al, Alec, Ali, Alick, Ally.

Alban:
From the Latin meaning "man from Alba," "blond," or "fair one," or from the English meaning "white." *Alternative spellings:* Alben, Albin, Albinus, Albyn, Alva, Elva.

Alberic:
From the German meaning "powerful elf." *Alternative spellings:* Alberich, Auberon, Aubrey, Oberon.

Albern:
From the German meaning "noble."

Albert:
From the Old English or German meaning "noble and bright." *Alternative spellings:* Alberk, Alberto, Albrik, Adelbert, Aliberto, Alvertos, Aubert, Bechtel, Elbert. *Short forms:* Al, Albie, Bert, Bertie, Berto, Berty.

Alberto:
The Italian form of Albert.

Albion:
From the Latin meaning "white cliffs."

Alden:
From the Old English meaning "old" or "wise protector."

Aldo:
From the Old German or Italian meaning "old and wise."

Aldous:
From the Germanic name Aldo, meaning "old." *Alternative spelling:* Eldon.

Aldrich:
From the Old English meaning an "old and wise ruler." *Alternative spellings:* Aldric, Aldridge, Audric, Eldredge, Eldridge, Elric. *Short forms:* Al, Rich.

Aldwin:
From the Old English meaning "wise and reliable friend."

Alec:
See Alexander.

Alejandro:
The Spanish form of Alexander.

Alessandro:
The Italian form of Alexander. *Short forms:* Alessio, Sandro.

Alex:
See Alexander. *Alternative spellings:* Alec, Alek, Alic, Alis.

A

Alexander:
From the Latin form of the Greek name Alexandros, from *alexin,* meaning "to defend," and *aner,* meaning "man or warrior," thus "man's defender and protector." *Alternative spellings:* Alecsandar, Alejandro, Alekos, Aleksandar, Aleksander, Aleksandr, Alessandro, Alexandar, Alexandor, Alexandr, Alexandre, Alexandros, Alexsander, Alexzander, Alisander, Alixander, Alixandre. *Short forms:* Al, Alec, Alek, Aleksi, Alex, Alexis, Alick, Ally, Lech, Lecks, Lex, Sacha, Sander, Sanders, Sandor, Sandy, Zander.

Alexandro:
The Greek form of Alexander.

Alexis:
Shortened form of Alexander.

Alfonso:
The Italian and Spanish form of Alphonse.

Alfred:
From the German and Old English meaning "good counsellor" or "elf counsellor." *Alternative spellings:* Alfeo, Alfredo, Alfric, Alfrick, Alfrid, Alfris, Alured, Avere, Avery, Elfrid. *Short forms:* Alf, Alfie, Fred, Freddie, Freddy.

Alfredo:
The Italian and Spanish form of Alfred.

Ali:
From the Arabic meaning "the god," "the highest," "the greatest."

Alijah:
A form of Elijah, meaning "the Lord is my God."

Alonso:
See Alphonse. *Alternative spellings:* Alonzo, Elonzo.

Alphonse:
From the German meaning "noble" or "eager." *Alternative spellings:* Alfonso, Alonzo, Alphons, Alphonso, Alphonsus. *Short forms:* Fonz, Fonzie, Lon, Lonnie.

Alvaro:
From the Spanish meaning "guardian."

Alvin:
From the German meaning "noble friend" or the Latin meaning "white" or "light skinned."

Amare:
From African origin, meaning "handsome, good looking."

Amari:
Of Arabic, Greek, Punjabi, German origin, meaning "immortal" or "builder."

Amarion:
See Omarion.

Amir:
From the Arabic meaning "prince."

Amos:
From the Hebrew meaning "burdened," "troubled."

Anderson:
From the Scandinavian meaning "son of Anders, son of Andrew."

Andre:
The French form of Andrew.

Andreas:
The Greek form of Andrew.

Andres:
The Spanish form of Andrew.

Andrew:
From the Greek meaning "manly." *Alternative spellings:* Adre, Andor, Andra, Andras, Andre, Andreas, Andrei, Andres, Anker, Druhan. *Short forms:* Andy, Drew.

Angel:
From the Greek meaning "angel" or the Latin meaning "messenger." *Alternative spellings:* Angelito, Angelo.

Angelo:
The Italian form of Angel.

Anthony:
From the Latin meaning "praiseworthy" or "priceless" or the Greek meaning "flourishing." *Alternative spellings:* Anthonu, Antjuan, Antoine, Antonio, Antony, Antwan. *Short forms:* Antal, Anton, Toni, Tony.

Antoine:
The French form of Anthony.

Antonio:
The Italian and Spanish form of Anthony.

A

Antwan:
The Arabic form of Anthony.

Ari:
A shortened form of Ariel, Arion, or Aristotle.

Ariel:
From the Hebrew meaning "lion of god." *Alternative spellings:* Ariell, Ariya, Ariyel, Arrial, Arriel. *Short forms:* Arel, Areli, Ari.

Arjun:
From the Sanskrit meaning "white."

Armand:
From the Latin meaning "noble" or the German meaning "soldier." *Alternative spellings:* Armad, Armando, Armands, Armani, Armon, Armondo.

Armando:
The Spanish form of Armand.

Armani:
From the Persian meaning "desire, goal." Also the Italian form of Armand and an Italian surname.

Arnav:
From the Sanskrit meaning "ocean, sea; stream, wave."

Arne:
From the Scandinavian meaning "eagle"; see also Arnold.

Arnold:
From the old German meaning "strength" or "eagle." *Alternative spellings:* Ardal, Arnaud, Arnault, Arnoll. *Short forms:* Arne, Arnie.

Aron:
See Aaron.

Arthur:
The origin of this name is disputed. It is either from the Irish meaning "noble" or "lofty hill"; the Celtic meaning "bear"; the Old English meaning "rock"; or the Icelandic meaning "follower of Thor." *Alternative spellings:* Artek, Arther, Arthor, Artor, Arturus, Artus, Aurthur. *Short forms:* Art, Arte, Arti, Artie, Arty.

Arturo:
The Italian form of Arthur.

Aryan:
From the Sanskrit meaning "warrior, honorable."

Asa:
From the Hebrew meaning "physician," "healer."

Asher:

From the Hebrew meaning "what happiness" or "blessed."

Ashley:

From the Old English meaning "ash tree meadow." *Alternative spellings: Ashleigh, Ashli, Ashlie, Ashly, Ashlyn.*

Athol:

From the Old English meaning "noble."

Atlas:

From the Greek meaning "lifted," "carried."

Atley:

From the Old English meaning "meadow."

Atticus:

From the Latin meaning "from Athens."

Attila:

From the Gothic meaning "little father."

Aubrey:

From the German meaning "noble" or "bearlike"; the French meaning "blond ruler"; or possibly English from French "elf ruler." *Alternative spellings: Aubree, Aubrie, Aubry, Aubury.*

Auden:

From the English meaning "old friend."

Augustine:

From the Latin meaning "majestic." *Alternative spellings: Agostino, Aguistin, Agustin, Austin. Short forms: August, Augie.*

Augustus:

From the Latin meaning "the exalted one."

Austin:

From the Latin meaning "the venerable one"; see also Augustine. *Alternative spelling: Austen.*

Avery:

From the old English meaning "ruler of the elfs."

Axel:

From the Latin meaning "ax"; the German meaning "small oak tree"; or the Scandinavian meaning "source of life" or "divine reward."

Aydan:

From the Turkish meaning "intelligence or attractive." *Alternative spellings: Ayden, Aydin.*

B

Bahir:
From the Arabic meaning "brilliant" or "dazzling."

Bailey:
From the French meaning "bailiff" or "steward" or the Middle English meaning "outer wall of a castle." *Alternative spellings:* Bailie, Baillie, Baily, Bayley, Bayly.

Baldrick:
From the German meaning "brave ruler" or "bold ruler." *Alternative spellings:* Baldric, Baudric.

Baldwin:
From the German meaning "bold friend." *Alternative spellings:* Balduin, Baldwyn, Baudoin.

Balfour:
From the Celtic meaning "pasture land" or the Old English meaning "distant hill."

Balthazar:
From the Greek meaning "may God protect the king." *Alternative spellings:* Baltasar, Balthasar, Belshazzar.

Balu:
From the Sanskrit meaning "young."

Barclay:
From the Celtic and Old English meaning "birch tree meadow." *Alternative spellings:* Barcley, Berkeley.

Barnabas:
From the Hebrew meaning "son of exhortation." *Alternative spellings:* Barnaby, Barnebus. *Short forms:* Barna, Barney, Barnie.

Barney:
From the Greek or Hebrew meaning "son of prophecy" or "consolation"; see also Barnabas.

Barnum:
From the German meaning "barn" or "storage place" or the English meaning "baron's home."

Baron:
From the Middle Latin meaning "man" or "warrior."

Barrett:
From the German meaning "strength of a bear."

Barry:
From the Old Celtic name Bearrach, meaning "spear" or "good marksman"; the Gaelic Irish name Fionnbharr, meaning "white haired," or the Welsh meaning "son of Harry." *Alternative spellings:* Barri, Barrie.

Bartholomew:
From the Aramaic meaning "son of Talmai." *Short forms:* Bart, Bartie.

Barton:
From the English *bere,* meaning "barley" and *tun,* meaning "enclosure," thus "barley farm."

Baruch:
From the Hebrew meaning "blessed."

Basil:
From the Greek *basileios,* meaning "kingly" or the Irish Gaelic meaning "war of strife." *Alternative spellings:* Basel, Basile, Bazil, Basilio, Basle, Vassily. *Short forms:* Bas, Baz.

Bassett:
From the English meaning "little person."

Beau:
From the French meaning "handsome," "beautiful." *Alternative spelling:* Bo.

Beaufort:
From the French meaning "beautiful fort."

Beaumont:
From the French meaning "beautiful mountain."

Beauregard:
From the French meaning "handsome," "beautiful," "well-regarded."

Beck:
From the Old Norse meaning "brook."

Beckett:
From the English meaning "dweller near the brook."

Bede:
From the Middle English meaning "prayer."

Bela:
From the Czech meaning "white" or the Hungarian meaning "bright."

Bellamy:
From the French meaning "beautiful friend."

B

Belvedere:
From the Italian meaning "beautiful to look at" or "a vantage point for a fine view." *Alternative spelling:* Belveder.

Ben:
From the Hebrew meaning "son" or the Scottish Gaelic meaning "peak"; see also Benedict and Benjamin.

Benedict:
From the Latin meaning "blessed." *Alternative spellings:* Bendick, Bendict, Benedik, Bendix, Benedetto, Benedicto, Benito, Benoit. *Short forms:* Ben, Beni.

Benjamin:
From the Hebrew meaning "son of my right hand." *Alternative spellings:* Bejamin, Beniam, Benjaman, Mincho. *Short forms:* Ben, Benjy, Benny.

Bennett:
From the Latin meaning "little one." *Alternative spelling:* Benoit.

Beno:
From the Hebrew meaning "son."

Benson:
From the English, meaning "son of Ben." See Ben. *Alternative spellings:* Bensen, Benssen, Bensson.

Bentley:
From the Old English meaning "moor," "coarse grass meadow."

Ben-Zion:
From the Hebrew meaning "son of Zion."

Beren:
Based on a name from Tolkien's *Lord of the Rings* that means "bearlike" or a shortened version of the Teutonic name Berenger.

Bernard:
From the German meaning "brave as a bear." *Alternative spellings:* Barnardo, Bearnard, Bernadas, Bernardin, Bernardo, Barnardus, Bernd, Bernek, Bernhard, Bjorn, Burnard. *Short forms:* Bern, Bernie, Berno.

Bert:
From the German meaning "bright"; also a short form of Albert and Berthold.

Berthold:
From the Old High German meaning "bright," "illustrious," or "brilliant ruler." *Alternative spellings:* Bertold, Bertolde, Bertus. *Short forms:* Bert, Bertie, Burt.

Bertram:
From the Old German meaning "bright" or "illustrious/bright raven."

Bertrand:
From the German meaning "bright shield."

Berwyn:
From the English meaning "harvest son."

Bevan:
From the Welsh meaning "son of Evan."

Beverly:
From the English meaning "beaver meadow." *Alternative spellings:* Beverlea, Beverley.

Bevis:
From the French meaning "bull."

Bill/Billy:
See William.

Birch:
From the English, meaning "bright or shining." *Alternative spellings:* Burch

Birgin:
From the Irish meaning "thin" or "lean" or the English meaning "river source." *Alternative spellings:* Blane, Blayne.

Birgir:
From the Norwegian meaning "rescued."

Bjorn:
From the Scandinavian, meaning "bear."

Blade:
From the English, meaning "knife, sword."

Blaine:
From the Irish meaning "thin, lean."

Blaise:
See Blaze.

Blake:
From the Old English meaning "dark meadow" or the Old Norse meaning "shining," "white."

Blaze:
From the Latin meaning "stammerer" or the English meaning "flame/trail mark." *Alternative spelling:* Blaise.

Blythe:
From the English meaning "carefree."

Bo:
Of Scandinavian origin, meaning "of life or living." Can be a nickname for boys and girls.

Boaz:
From the Hebrew meaning "swift" or "strong." *Alternative spellings:* Bo, Bos, Boz.

Bob/Bobby:
See Robert.

Boden:
From the Scandinavian meaning "sheltered" or the French meaning "messenger" or "herald."

Borak:
From the Arabic or Hebrew meaning "lightning."

Borg:
From the Scandinavian meaning "castle."

Boris:
From the Slavic meaning "battler" or "warrior" or the Russian meaning "fight."

Boston:
From the Middle English meaning "town by the woods." A city in Massachusetts.

Bourne:
From the Latin or French meaning "boundary" or the English meaning "brook," "stream."

Boyce:
From the French, meaning "forest."

Boyd:
From the Celtic meaning "yellow-haired."

Brad:
Short form of names beginning with Brad.

Bradley:
From the Old English meaning "broad meadow." *Short form:* Brad.

Brady:
From the Irish meaning "spirited" or the English meaning "broad island."

Braeden:
See Braden.

Bram:
From the Celtic meaning "bramble"; also a diminutive form of Abraham.

Brandeis:
From the Czech meaning "dweller on a burned clearing."

Brandon:
From the Old English *brom* and *dun,* meaning "gorse hill" or "beacon hill." *Alternative spellings:* Brandan, Brandin, Brannon. *Short forms:* Bran, Brand.

Branson:
From the English, meaning "son of Brand".

Braxton:
From the Old English meaning "brock's town." Brock is an informal word for "badger."

Brayan:
See Brian.

Brayden:
From the English meaning "from the wide valley." *Alternative spellings:* Bradan, Bradden, Braddon, Braden, Bradin, Bradon, Bradyn, Braeden, Braedon, Braiden, Braidin, Braydon

Braylen:
A contemporary invented name. Possible link to Brayden or Brandon.

Brede:
From the Scandinavian meaning "iceberg," "glacier."

Brendan:
From the Irish meaning "little raven" or the Gaelic meaning "prince." *Alternative spellings:* Brenden, Brendon, Bryn.

Brennan:
From the Irish meaning "descendent of the sad one." *Alternative spelling:* Brennen.

Brent:
From the Old English meaning "steep hill." *Alternative spelling:* Brenton.

Brett:
From the Gaelic meaning "Great Britain" or the Old French meaning "a person from Brittany." *Alternative spellings:* Brit, Brittain, Brittan, Britten.

Brian:
From the Irish Gaelic meaning "strong," "virtuous," or "honourable" or the Greek meaning "strong." *Alternative spellings:* Brano, Briant, Brin, Briny, Brion, Bryan, Bryant, Bryon.

Brice:
From the Welsh meaning "alert" or "ambitious"; the English meaning "son of Rice" or "son of the ardent one"; or the Celtic meaning "strong" or "brave." *Alternative spelling:* Bryce.

Brock:
From the Old English *broc,* meaning "badger."

B

Broderick:
From the Welsh meaning "son of the famous ruler"; the English meaning "broad ridge"; or the Celtic meaning "brother." *Alternative spellings:* Broderic, Brodric, Brodrick. *Short form:* Brod.

Brody:
From the Irish meaning "ditch/canal builder"; also a pet form of the Scandinavian name Broder, meaning "brother." *Alternative spellings:* Brodi, Brodie.

Bronson:
From the English meaning "son of Brown."

Brook:
From the English meaning "brook," "stream."

Brooklyn:
From the area of New York City.

Brosnan:
From the Irish Gaelic meaning "one from Brosna" in Ireland or "dweller near the Brosna River."

Bruce:
From the Old French meaning "brushwood thicket," "woods."

Bruno:
From Old German *brun,* meaning "brown."

Brutus:
From the Latin meaning "heavy," "irrational," "stupid," or "unreasonable."

Bryan:
See Brian.

Bryant:
See Brian.

Bryce:
See Brice.

Brynmor:
From the Welsh meaning "great hill."

Bryson:
From the Welsh *brych,* meaning "speckled." *Alternative spelling:* Brycen.

Bud:
From the English meaning "herald," "messenger."

Byron:
Derived from the English word "bust," from burst.

C

Cade:
From the Old English meaning "round, stout cask or barrel." *Alternative spelling:* Kade.

Caden:
A contemporary invented name. *Alternative spellings:* Caiden, Cayden, Kadin, Kadyn, Kaeden, Kaiden, Kayden.

Cadmus:
From the Greek meaning "from the east."

Cadogan:
From the Old Welsh meaning "battle glory."

Cael:
See Cale.

Cahan:
See Kane.

Cahil:
From the Turkish meaning "young native."

Cain:
See Kane.

Cairn:
From the Welsh meaning "landmark piled up with stones."

Caius:
From the Latin meaning "rejoice."

Caldwell:
From the English meaning "cold well."

Cale:
From the Hebrew, a short form of Caleb. *Alternative spellings:* Cael, Cail, Kale.

Caleb:
From the Hebrew meaning "bold, intrepid." *Alternative spelling:* Kaleb. *Short form:* Cale.

Calhoun:
From the Irish meaning "narrow woods" or the Scottish meaning "warrior."

Callum:
From the Gaelic meaning "dove." *Alternative spelling:* Calum.

C

Calvin:
From the French or Latin meaning "little bald one."

Camden:
From the Scottish meaning "winding valley."

Cameron:
From the Gaelic meaning "crooked nose." *Alternative spellings:* Camren, Camron, Camryn.

Campbell:
From the Celtic meaning "curved" or "crooked mouth" or the Latin meaning "beautiful field."

Cannon:
From French origin, meaning "official of the church." Not related to firearms.

Canute:
From the Latin meaning "white-haired" or the Scandinavian meaning "knot."

Carl:
See Charles. *Alternative spellings:* Carlos, Karl.

Carlo:
The Italian form of Charles.

Carlos:
The Spanish form of Charles.

Carlton:
From the Old English meaning "settlement of the [free] peasants."

Carmelo:
From Italian and Hebrew origin, meaning "fruitful orchard; garden." *Alternative spellings:* Carmel, Carmeli, Carmello, Karmelo, Karmello.

Carmine:
From the Latin meaning "song" or "crimson."

Carney:
From the Irish meaning "victorious" or the Scottish meaning "fighter."

Carson:
From the Gaelic meaning "son of the marsh dwellers."

Carter:
From the English meaning "cart driver."

Cary:
From the Greek meaning "pure." *Alternative spelling:* Carey.

Case
Familiar form of Casey.

Casey:
From the Celtic meaning "brave in battle." *Short form:* Case.

Cash:
Short form of Cassius, from the Latin meaning "vain."

Casimir:
From the Slavic meaning "peace-maker." *Alternative spellings:* Casimer, Kazimir, Kazmer. *Short form:* Cass.

Cason:
Of contemporary origin. An invented name, possibly a form of Jason.

Caspar:
From the German meaning "imperial." *Alternative spellings:* Casper, Gaspar, Jaspar, Kaspa, Kaspar, Kasper.

Cassius:
From the Latin meaning "box" or "protective cover."

Castor:
From the Greek meaning "beaver."

Cathal:
From the Irish Gaelic meaning "battle mighty."

Cayden:
See Caden.

Cecil:
From the Latin meaning "blind."

Cedric:
From the Celtic meaning "model of generosity." *Alternative spelling:* Cerdic.

Cemlyn:
From the Welsh meaning "bent lake."

Ceri:
From the Welsh meaning "love."

Cesar:
The Spanish form of Caesar, from the Latin meaning "long haired."

Chad:
From the English meaning "warrior."

Chadwick:
From the Old English meaning "dairy farm" or "warrior's farm."

Chaim:
From the Hebrew meaning "life."

C

Chance:
From the Old English meaning "good fortune."

Chandler:
From the Old French meaning "candle maker."

Charles:
From the Old German meaning "free man." *Alternative spellings:* Carl, Carlos, Karl. *Short forms:* Charlie, Chaz.

Charlie:
See Charles.

Chase:
From the Old French meaning "huntsman."

Chaz:
See Charles.

Chet:
From the Thai meaning "brother."

Chevy:
From the French *chevalier,* meaning "horseman" or "knight."

Chris:
See Christopher or Christian.

Christian:
From the Latin meaning the "follower of Christ." *Alternative spellings:* Christiano, Christianos, Christiao, Christien, Chrystian, Cristian, Crysek, Krist, Krista, Kristian, Kristos, Krysek, Krystian. *Short forms:* Chris, Christie, Christy, Chrys, Kris, Kristie, Kristy, Krys.

Christie:
See Christopher or Christian.

Christopher:
From the Greek *christoforus,* meaning "the bearer of Christ." *Alternative spellings:* Christofer, Christoffer, Christoforus, Christophe, Cristobad, Kristofer, Kristoffer, Kristopher. *Short forms:* Chris, Christie, Cris, Cristo, Cristof, Kit, Kris, Kriss.

Cian:
From the Irish Gaelic meaning "ancient."

Ciaran:
From the Irish Gaelic meaning "black." *Alternative spellings:* Ciaron, Kieran, Kieron.

Cid:
From the Spanish meaning "lord." *Alternative spellings:* Sid, Cyd.

Cillian:
From the Irish Gaelic meaning "strife," "monastery," or "church."

Clancy:
From the Irish Gaelic meaning "red warrior."

Clarence:
From the Latin meaning "clear" or "victorious."

Clark:
From the Old English meaning "learned man." *Alternative spelling:* Clarke.

Claude:
From the Latin meaning "lame." *Alternative spellings:* Claud, Claudius.

Clayton:
From the Old English meaning "clay enclosure" or "settlement in the clay." *Short form:* Clay.

Clement:
From the Latin meaning "mild" or "merciful." *Alternative spellings:* Clem, Clemence, Clemente, Clemento, Klement. *Short forms:* Clem, Clemmie.

Clifford:
From the Old English meaning "ford by the slope." *Short form:* Cliff.

Clifton:
From the Old English meaning "settlement on the slope."

Clinton:
From the Middle English meaning "hilltop town." *Short form:* Clint.

Clive:
From the Old English meaning "steep/high rock face."

Clyde:
From the Welsh meaning "heard from far away" or "warm."

Coby:
Familiar form of Jacob.

Cody:
From the Irish meaning "helpful person." *Alternative spellings:* Codi, Codie, Kody.

Cohen:
From the Hebrew meaning "priest."

Colbert:
From the Old French meaning "bright" or "famous."

C

Colby:
Possibly from the Old English meaning "dark," "dark-haired"; *berht,* meaning "famous," or the Gaelic *colla,* meaning "high."

Cole:
From the Old English meaning "charcoal" or the Latin meaning "cabbage farmer."

Coleman:
From the Anglo Saxon meaning "follower of the doves"; the Middle English meaning "coal miner"; or the Latin meaning "cabbage farmer."

Colin:
From the Gaelic meaning "youth"; see also Nicholas. *Alternative spelling:* Collin.

Coll:
From the Old Celtic meaning "high."

Colm:
From the Irish meaning "dove."

Colt:
From the Old English meaning "young male horse; frisky." Also familiar form of Colton.

Colton:
From the English meaning "from the black coal town." *Alternative spellings:* Coltan, Colten, Coltin, Kolton.

Conall:
From the Old Celtic meaning "strong wolf" or the Celtic meaning "high and mighty." *Alternative spelling:* Conal.

Conan:
From the Gaelic meaning "wolf"; the Celtic meaning "high" or "wisdom"; or the Old Irish meaning "lover of hounds."

Conley:
From the Gaelic meaning "pure."

Conn:
From the Irish Gaelic meaning "chief."

Connor:
From the Gaelic name Conchobhar, meaning "high desire" or the Celtic meaning "wise." *Alternative spelling:* Conner.

Conrad:
From the German meaning "bold in counsel"; see also Curtis. *Alternative spellings:* Conrade, Conrado, Konrad. *Short forms:* Con, Connie, Conny, Cort, Curt, Kurt.

Constant:
From the Latin meaning "remain steadfast in faith." *Alternative spelling:* Constantine.

Cooper:
From the English meaning "a man who makes barrels."

Corbin:
From the Anglo-Norman meaning "crow." *Alternative spelling:* Corbinian.

Corcy:
Possibly from the Irish meaning "good peace" or "hollow." *Alternative spelling:* Cory.

Corin:
From the Roman god Quirinus.

Cormac:
From the Irish Gaelic meaning "charioteer"; the Greek meaning "tree trunk"; or the Irish meaning "raven's son."

Cornelius:
From the Latin meaning "horn." *Short form:* Cornell.

Cortez:
From the Spanish meaning "in triumph; courteous."

Cory:
See Corey.

Craig:
From the Celtic meaning "rock."

Cristian:
See Christian.

Cristobal:
The Spanish form of Christopher.

Cristofer:
See Christopher.

Cruz:
From the Spanish meaning "cross."

Cullen:
From the Irish and Gaelic meaning "good-looking boy, handsome."

Curtis:
From the Old French meaning "courteous." *Alternative spelling:* Conrad. *Short forms:* Curt, Kurt.

Cyril:
From the Classic Greek meaning "lord."

Cyrus:
From the Greek meaning "Lord" or the Persian meaning "sun" or "throne."

C

D

Dagan:
From the Hebrew meaning "corn" or "grain" or the Babylonian meaning "little fish."

Dakota:
From the Native American Sioux meaning "friend."

Dale:
From the Old Norse meaning "broad valley," "hollow."

Dallas:
From the Scottish meaning "from the dales, the valley meadows." A city in Texas.

Dalton:
From the Old English meaning "from the hamlet in the valley."

Daly:
From the Irish, meaning "assembly." *Alternative spelling:* Daley.

Dalziel:
From the Scottish meaning "small field."

Damarion:
Of contemporary origin. An invented name, combining Da and Marion. *Alternative spelling:* Demarion.

Damian:
From the Greek meaning "to tame/kill" or "tamer of men." *Alternative spellings:* Damien, Damion.

Damon:
From the Greek meaning "divine power" or "fate" or the Old English *doeg,* meaning "day."

Dan:
See Daniel.

Dandre:
Of contemporary origin. An invented name combining D and Andre. A form of Andre. *Alternative spelling:* Deandre.

Dane:
From the Old Norse meaning "Danish"; see also Daniel.

Dangelo:

Of contemporary origin. An invented name combining D and Angelo. *Alternative spellings:* D'Angelo. DeAngelo.

Daniel:

From the Hebrew meaning "God has judged." *Alternative spellings:* Daneil, Danek, Daniela, Danil, Danya. *Short forms:* Dan, Dana, Dane, Danek, Danko, Dannie, Dano, Danny, Donal.

Dante:

From the Italian meaning "to endure," "to last."

Darby:

From the Old Norse meaning "one from the deer estate" or the Irish Gaelic meaning "a free man." *Alternative spellings:* Derby, Diarmaid.

Darcy:

From the Irish Gaelic meaning "a dark man."

Darian:

A contemporary form of Darius. *Alternative spelling:* Darien.

Dario:

The Italian form of Darius.

Darion:

See Darren.

Darius:

From the Greek meaning "prosperous" or "rich" or the Latin *daraya,* meaning "to possess." *Alternative spelling:* Darrius. *Short forms:* Dario, Deny.

Darnell:

From the Old English meaning "from the hidden/secret nook."

Darrell:

From the Old English meaning "darling," "dear," "beloved," "special." *Alternative spellings:* Darel, Darrel, Darryl, Derril.

Darren:

From the Irish meaning "dearly beloved" or "small and great" or the Greek meaning "wealthy." *Alternative spellings:* Darien, Darin, Dario, Daron, Darran.

Darrick:

See Derek.

Darrow:

From the Old English meaning "spear."

Darryl:

See Darrel.

D

Darshan:
From the Sanskrit meaning "to see."

Darwin:
From the Old English meaning "lover of the sea" or "beloved friend."

Dashawn:
Of contemporary origin. An invented name combining Da and Shawn. *Alternative spellings:* Dashaun, Deshaun.

Davian:
A contemporary invented name. *Alternative spelling:* Davion.

David:
From the Hebrew meaning "beloved." *Alternative spellings:* Davide, Davin, Davis, Dawe, Dawes, Dawson, Devi, Dewi, Dov, Dow. *Short forms:* Dave, Davey, Davi, Davy, Tab.

Davis:
From the Welsh meaning "son of David."

Davon:
A contemporary invented name. *Alternative spellings:* Daven, Daveon, Davin, Davion, Davonn, Davyn, Davyon, Deavon.

Dawson:
From the Old English meaning "son of David."

Dax:
From the town in Western France.

Daxton:
A contemporary invented name. A variant of Dax.

Dayton:
From the English meaning "bright and sunny town."

Deacon:
From the Greek meaning "servant."

Dean:
Possibly from the Old English meaning "valley" or the Latin meaning "leader of ten." *Short form:* Dino.

Deandre:
See Dandre.

Deangelo:
See Dangelo.

Decimus:
From the Latin meaning "tenth."

Declan:

Possibly from the Irish meaning "son of prayer."

Deepak:

From the Sanskrit meaning "little lamp" or "shining"; also the Hindu god of love.

Delany:

From the Irish Gaelic meaning "the challenger's descendant."

Delmar:

From the Latin meaning "from the sea."

Delroy:

From the French meaning "belonging to the king."

Demarcus:

Of contemporary origin. An invented name combining De and Marcus.

Demarion:

See Damarion.

Demetrius:

From Greek origin, meaning "lover of the earth, given to the Earth goddess" *Alternative spellings:* Dametrius, Demetris, Demitrios, Demitrius, Dhimitrios, Dimitrios. *Short forms:* Dimitri

Dempsey:

From the Middle English meaning "absence of merit," "deserving of blame."

Denholm:

Possibly from the Scottish meaning "place" or "island valley."

Dennis:

See Dionysus. *Alternative spellings:* Denis, Dennes, Dennys. *Short forms:* Den, Denny.

Denver:

From the French, meaning "green valley."

Denzel:

Possibly from the Celtic meaning "stronghold" or the Old English meaning "high." *Alternative spelling:* Denzil.

Deon:

See Dion.

Derek:

From the Old German meaning "the people's ruler." *Alternative spellings:* Darrick, Dereck, Derick, Derrick, Dirk.

Dereon:

See Dorian.

D

Deshaun:
See Dashawn.

Desmond:
From the Latin *mundus,* meaning "the universe," "the heavens," "the earth," or "mankind."

Dev:
From the Sanskrit meaning "god."

Devan:
See Devon.

Deven:
See Devon.

Devin:
From the Irish meaning "poet." *Alternative spelling:* Devyn.

Devlin:
From the Irish meaning "misfortune."

Devon:
From the English county. *Alternative spellings:* Devan, Deven, Devonte.

Devonte:
See Devon.

Devyn:
See Devin.

Dewey:
From the Welsh meaning "beloved." *Alternative spelling:* Dewi.

Dewi:
See David or Dewey.

Dewitt:
From the Flemish meaning "blond."

Dexter:
From the Latin meaning "right-handed." *Short form:* Dex.

Deyla:
From the Norse meaning "compassionate."

Diarmuid:
See Dermot. *Alternative spelling:* Diarmid.

Didier:
From the Latin meaning "desired." *Short form:* Didi.

Diego:
The Spanish form of James.

Dillan:

From the Irish Gaelic meaning "faithful."
Alternative spellings: Dilan, Dillon, Dylan.

Dimitri:

See Demetrius.

Dino:

From the German meaning "little sword"; see also Dean.

Dinsdale:

From the Irish Gaelic meaning "settlement surrounded by a moat."

Dinsmore:

From the Irish Gaelic meaning "fortified hill."

Dion:

From the Greek meaning "child of Heaven." Also diminutive of Dionysus.

Dionysus:

From the Greek god of wine. *Alternative spellings:* Donis, Donnes, Dionis, Dioniso, Dwight. *Short forms:* Den, Denny, Dio, Dion.

Dirk:

See Derek.

Dixon:

See Richard.

Dodi:

From the Hebrew meaning "beloved."
Alternative spelling: Dodo.

Dolan:

From the Irish meaning "dark-haired."

Dolph:

See Randolph.

Dominic:

From the Latin *dominicus,* meaning "belonging to a lord or master" or "servant of God." *Alternative spellings:* Domenic, Domingo, Dominick, Dominik, Dominique. *Short forms:* Dom, Don, Nic, Nick, Nickie, Nicky.

Donahue:

From the Irish Gaelic meaning "dark warrior."

Donal:

From the Gaelic meaning "world mighty."

Donald:

From the Celtic name Domhnall, meaning "world" or "mighty."
Alternative spelling: Donaldo. *Short forms:* Don, Donal, Doni, Donnie, Donny.

D

Donatus:
From the Latin meaning "given," "bestowed upon." *Alternative spellings:* Donat, Donato. *Short forms:* Don, Doni, Donnie, Donny.

Donnel:
From the Gaelic meaning "hill" or "hill-fort."

Donnelly:
From the Celtic meaning "brave" or "dark/black man."

Donovan:
From the Celtic meaning "dark" or "brown-haired warrior." *Alternative spelling:* Donavan. *Short forms:* Don, Donnie, Donny, Van.

Donte:
See Dante.

Dooley:
From the Irish meaning "dark hero."

Dorian:
From the Greek *dorios,* meaning "child of the sea"; see also Doran.

Dorran:
From the Celtic meaning "strange" or the Greek meaning "a gift."

Dorsey:
Probably from the French d'Orsay, meaning "from Orsay."

Doug:
See Dougal or Douglas.

Dougal:
From the Celtic name Dugald meaning "dark stranger." *Short form:* Doug.

Douglas:
From the Celtic meaning "dark water," "dark stream." *Short form:* Doug.

Dov:
From the Hebrew meaning "bear"; see also David.

Doyle:
From the Irish meaning "assembly," "gathering."

Drake:

From the Gaelic meaning "dragon" or the Greek meaning "serpent."

Draven:

A contemporary invented name.

Drew:

See Andrew.

Driscoll:

From the Celtic meaning "sad," "distressed."

Druhan:

See Andrew.

Dryden:

From the Middle English meaning "dry secluded valley."

Duane:

From the Gaelic meaning "black," "dark." *Alternative spellings:* Duayne, Dwane, Dwayne.

Dudley:

From the Old English meaning "Dudo's meadow."

Dugan:

From the Irish Gaelic meaning "small and dark."

Duke:

From the Latin *dux,* meaning "leader," "conductor," "guide," "commander."

Dumont:

From the French meaning "from the mountain/hill."

Duncan:

From the Celtic meaning "brown warrior," "dark-skinned warrior."

Dustin:

From the Old German meaning "fighter" or the Old Norse meaning "Thor's stone." *Short forms:* Dust, Dustie, Dusty.

Dwayne:

From the Irish and Gaelic meaning "swarthy or dark." *Alternative spellings:* Dawayne, Dewayne, Duane, Duwain, Duwayne, Dwain, Dwaine, Dwane.

Dwight:

From the Old English or Old Dutch meaning "white" or "fair" or the French version of "Dionysus."

Dylan:

From the Welsh meaning "son of the waves." *Alternative spelling:* Dillon.

E

Eagan:
From the Irish meaning "fiery," "forceful." *Alternative spellings:* Egan, Egon.

Eamon:
An Irish form of Edmund. *Alternative spelling:* Eamonn.

Ean:
See Ian.

Earl:
From the Old English meaning "nobleman" or "chief." *Alternative spelling:* Errol.

Easton:
From the English, meaning "from East town."

Eben:
From the Hebrew meaning "rock," "stone."

Ebner:
See Abner.

Edan:
From the Celtic meaning "flame," "fire."

Eddie:
See Edward. *Alternative spelling:* Eddy.

Eden:
From the Hebrew meaning "delight."

Edgar:
From the Old English meaning "happy spear." *Alternative spelling:* Adair. *Short forms:* Ed, Eddie, Eddy.

Edison:
From the English meaning "son of Edward." *Alternative spelling:* Edson.

Edmund:
From the Old English meaning "happy protection" or "happy guardian." *Alternative spellings:* Eamon, Eamonn, Edmond, Edmondo, Edmundo. *Short forms:* Ed, Ned, Neddie, Ted, Teddy.

Edoardo:
The Italian form of Edward.

Edom:

From the Hebrew meaning "red."

Edson:

See Edison.

Eduardo:

The Spanish form of Edward.

Edward:

From the Old English meaning "rich guardian" or "happy protector." *Alternative spellings:* Edoardo, Edorta, Edouard, Eduard, Eduardo, Edvard, Edvardo, Edwardo. *Short forms:* Ed, Eddie, Eddy, Edo, Edwy, Ned, Neddy, Ted, Teddy.

Edwin:

From the Old English meaning "rich friend." *Short form:* Ed.

Efrain:

The Spanish variant of Ephraim. *Alternative spelling:* Efren.

Egan:

From the Irish Gaelic meaning "small fiery one."

Egbert:

From the English meaning "shining sword," "bright sword."

Egerton:

From the Middle English meaning "corner of the town" or the English meaning "Edgar's town."

Egmont:

From the Middle English meaning "corner of the hill."

Egor:

See George or Igor.

Eifion:

From the Welsh meaning "place name."

Eilir:

From the Welsh meaning "butterfly."

Einar:

From the Old Norse meaning "individualist" or "lone warrior."

Eion:

See Ian.

Elan:

From the Hebrew meaning "tree" or the Latin meaning "spirited."

Elazar:

From the Hebrew meaning "God helped." *Alternative spellings:* Elazaro, Elazer, Eleazar, Eliezer, Elizar.

E

Eldon:
See Aldous.

Elgar:
From the Old English meaning "noble spear."

Elgin:
From the Old English *aethel,* meaning "noble," and the Celtic *gwen,* meaning "white," "pure."

Eli:
From the Hebrew meaning "height." *Alternative spelling:* Ely.

Elian:
See Elijah.

Elias:
See Elijah.

Eliezer:
See Elazar.

Elihu:
See Eliyahu.

Elijah:
From the Hebrew meaning "faithful to God," "the Lord is my God." *Alternative spellings:* Elian, Elias, Elliot, Ellis. *Short form:* Eli.

Eliseo:
The Italian and Spanish form of Elisha.

Elisha:
From the Hebrew meaning "God is my help," "God is generous." *Short form:* Eli.

Eliyahu:
From the Hebrew meaning "the Lord is my God." *Alternative spelling:* Elihu. *Short form:* Eli.

Ellery:
From the English meaning "elder tree island."

Elliot:
See Elijah. *Alternative spellings:* Eliot, Elliott.

Ellis:
See Elijah.

Ellison:
From the Old English meaning "son of Ellis."

Ellwood:
From the English, meaning "nobleman's wood." *Alternative spelling:* Elwood.

Elmer:
From the English meaning "noble," "famous." *Alternative spellings:* Aylmer, Ellmer, Elmo.

Elmo:
See Elmer or Erasmus.

Elonzo:
See Alonso.

Eloy:
From the Latin meaning "chosen one."

Elrad:
From the English meaning "noble counsel."

Elroy:
From the Spanish meaning "the king."

Elston:
From the Old English meaning "the noble's town" or "noble town." *Alternative spelling:* Elton.

Elton:
Possibly from the Old English meaning "old town"; see also Elston.

Elvin:
From the Old High German meaning "elf like," "quick-witted," or "clever friend." *Alternative spelling:* Elvis.

Elvis:
Possibly from the Scandinavian meaning "wise" or the Old Norse meaning "all-knowing"; see also Elvin.

Elwyn:
From the Welsh meaning "white brow."

Emanuel:
From the Hebrew meaning "God is with us." *Alternative spelling:* Emmanuel. *Short forms:* Manu, Manuel.

Emerson:
From the German or English meaning "son of Emery."

Emery:
From the Old High German meaning "ruler," "power," or "wealth." *Alternative spellings:* Almery, Amory, Emerick, Emerson, Emil, Emile, Emilio, Emlin, Emlyn, Emmerich, Emmerlich, Emory.

Emil:
From the Latin meaning "flatterer" or the German meaning "industrious." *Alternative spellings:* Emile, Émile, Emill.

Emiliano:
The Spanish form of Emil.

E

Emilio:
The Spanish or Italian form of Emil.

Emlyn:
See Emery or Emil.

Emmanuel:
See Emanuel.

Emmet:
From the Hebrew meaning "truth."

Emory:
See Emery.

Emrys:
From the Greek meaning "immortal."

Eneas:
From the Greek name Aeneas, meaning "praised."

Engelbert:
From the Old German meaning "bright as an angel."

Ennis:
From the Greek meaning "mine"; see also Angus.

Enoch:
From the Hebrew meaning "dedicated" or "educated."

Enos:
From the Hebrew meaning "man."

Enrique:
Spanish meaning "ruler of a home" or "estate/heir/person of a high rank"; see also Henry.

Enzo:
The Italian form of Henry. Also diminutive of Lorenzo and Vicenzo.

Eoghan:
From the Gaelic meaning "born of dew"; see also Eugene.

Eoin:
See John.

Ephraim:
From the Hebrew, meaning "fertile or productive." *Alternative spelling:* Efraim.

Erasmus:
From the Greek *erasmios,* meaning "loved," "desired." *Short form:* Elmo.

Erhard:
From the Old German meaning "resolution."

Eric:
From the Old Norse meaning "sole ruler." *Alternative spellings:* Erick, Erik. *Short forms:* Ric, Rick.

Erin:
From the Gaelic Éirinn, meaning "Ireland." *Alternative spelling:* Ayrin.

Ernest:
From the Old German meaning "vigor" or "earnestness." *Alternative spellings:* Earnest, Ernestino, Ernesto, Ernestus. *Short forms:* Ernie, Erno, Ernst.

Ernesto:
The Spanish form of Ernest.

Ernst:
See Ernest.

Errol:
From the Latin meaning "wanderer"; see also Earl.

Erskine:
From the Scottish meaning "green ascent" or the Gaelic meaning "from the height of the cliff."

Erwin:
From the Old English meaning "sea friend."

Eryl:
From the Welsh meaning "watcher."

Esau:
From the Hebrew meaning "hairy."

Esmund:
From the Old English meaning "very good" or "gracious protector." *Alternative spelling:* Esmond.

Esteban:
See Stephen.

Estevan
The Spanish form of Stephen.

E

Ethan:
From the Hebrew meaning "constant," "permanent," "long-lived," or "strong." *Alternative spelling:* Ethen.

Ethelbert:
From the Old English name Aethelbryht, which is from *aethel,* meaning "noble," and *beorht,* meaning "bright."

Ethelred:
From the Old English meaning "noble strength."

Etienne:
The French form of Stephen.

Eugene:
From the Greek meaning "well born." *Alternative spellings:* Eoghan, Evgeny. *Short form:* Gene.

Eunan:
From the Gaelic meaning "great fear" or "little horror" or possibly from Adam.

Eurig:
From the Welsh meaning "gold."

Eustace:
From the Greek meaning "rich in corn." *Short form:* Stacey.

Evan:
From the Irish meaning "young warrior"; see also John. *Alternative spellings:* Ian, Euan, Ewan, Yves. *Short form:* Van.

Evander:
From the Greek, meaning "good man." *Short form:* Vander.

Evelyn:
From the Old English meaning "hazelnut."

Everard:
From the Old High German meaning "strong warrior."

Everett:
From the Old English meaning "strong boar."

Ewan:
See Ewen or John.

Ezekiel:
From the Hebrew meaning "strength of God." *Alternative spellings:* Esequiel, Ezechiel, Ezequiel, Eziechiele, Eziequel, Zeke.

Ezra:
From the Hebrew meaning "help."

F

Fabian:
From the Latin meaning "bean grower."
Alternative spellings: Fabien, Fabioano.
Short forms: Faber, Fabio.

Fabrizio:
From the Italian meaning "craftsman."

Faine:
From the Old English meaning "good-natured." *Alternative spelling:* Fane.

Falco:
From the German meaning "people" or "tribe" or the Latin meaning "falconer."
Alternative spellings: Falk, Falke, Falken.

Farley:
From the Old English meaning "fair meadow."

Farquhar:
From the Gaelic meaning "friendly man."

Farran:
From the Irish meaning "the land."

Faust:
From the Latin meaning "lucky," "fortunate." *Alternative spelling:* Faustus.

Favian:
From the Latin meaning "understanding."

Federico:
From the Spanish or Italian meaning "peaceful ruler."

Felipe:
The Spanish form of Philip.

Felix:
From the Latin meaning "happy."
Alternative spellings: Fela, Felex, Felic, Felicks, Felixiano.

Fenn:
From the Old English meaning "marsh."

Fergal:
From the Irish meaning "man of strength."

Fernando:
From the Spanish meaning "adventurer."
Alternative spelling: Fernand.

F

Ferris:
The Irish Gaelic form of Peter.

Festus:
From the German meaning "festive," "joyful," "merry."

Finaly:
From the Scottish meaning "fair hero."

Finan:
From the Irish Gaelic meaning "little and fair." *Alternative spelling:* Finian.

Finbar:
From the Gaelic meaning "fair head."

Fingal:
From the Gaelic meaning "fair stranger."

Finlay:
From the Gaelic meaning "a sunbeam" or "small, fair-haired brave one." *Alternative spellings:* Findlay, Findley, Finley. *Short forms:* Fin, Finn.

Finn:
From the Gaelic meaning "light skinned, fair"; see also Finlay, Finnegan.

Finnegan:
From the Gaelic meaning "light skinned, fair." *Short forms:* Fin, Finn.

Finnian:
From the Gaelic meaning "fair." *Alternative spelling:* Finnigan.

Fintan:
From the Old Irish meaning "white," "fair" or possibly "brave." *Alternative spelling:* Fiontan.

Fisher:
From the English meaning "one who fishes."

Fisk:
From the German meaning "fish."

Fitz:
From the Old English meaning "son."

Flavio:
From the Latin meaning "blond" or "tawny."

Fletcher:
From the English meaning "maker of arrows.

Florian:
From the Slavic or Latin meaning "flower."

Floyd:
See Lloyd.

Flynn:
From the Irish meaning "son of a red-haired man." *Alternative spellings:* Flin, Flinn, Flyn.

Fonzie:
See Alphonso.

Ford:
From the English meaning "shallow place to cross water."

Forrest:
From the Middle English meaning "forest protector."

Foster:
From the English meaning "forest ranger."

Francesco:
The Italian form of Francis.

Francis:
From the Latin meaning "free man" or "Frenchman." *Alternative spellings:* Francesco, Francisco, François, Pancho, Paquito. *Short forms:* Franc, Frank, Frankie, Franky, Frans.

Francisco:
The Spanish form of Francis.

François:
French form of Francis.

Frank:
From the English meaning "freeman" or possibly from a fourth-century tribe that migrated to Gaul, meaning "Frenchman." *Short forms:* Franki, Frankie, Franky.

Franklin:
From the English meaning "landholder," "freeman." *Alternative spelling:* Franklyn. *Short form:* Frank.

Fraiser:
From the Old English meaning "curly haired" or the Old French meaning "strawberry." *Alternative spellings:* Fraser, Frazer, Frazier.

Freddy:
Short form of names containing "fred," such as Frederick and Alfred.

Frederick:
From the Old German meaning "peaceful ruler." *Alternative spellings:* Federico, Fredrick, Friedrich, Fritz. *Short forms:* Fred, Freddie, Freddy, Ric, Rick, Rickie, Ricky.

G

Gabriel:
From the Hebrew meaning "man of God," "God's able-bodied one." *Alternative spellings:* Gabrial, Gabriele, Gabrielle. *Short forms:* Gab, Gabby, Gabe, Gabie, Gabor.

Gael:
From the Irish meaning "Gaelic speaking Celt."

Gage:
From the Old French meaning "pledge, oath." *Alternative spellings:* Gaige, Gauge.

Gaige:
See Gage.

Gareth:
From the Welsh meaning "gentle."

Garfield:
From the Old English meaning "spearfield."

Garrett:
The Irish form of Gerard. *Alternative spellings:* Garet, Garett, Garritt, Gerrit.

Garrison:
From the English meaning "son of Garrett." It is also the name for a military barracks or fortification.

Garth:
From the Scandinavian meaning "garden" or the Old Norse meaning "enclosure," "from the garden" or "protection."

Gary:
From the Old English *gar,* meaning "spear," or *gari,* meaning "spear man." *Alternative spelling:* Garry.

Gauge:
See Gage.

Gaven:
See Gavin.

Gavin:
From the Welsh meaning "hawk of the plain" or "white hawk." *Alternative spellings:* Gaven, Gavyn, Gawain, Gawaine, Gawin.

Gene:
See Eugene.

Geoffrey:
From the Old German meaning "district" or "peace" or the English meaning "peaceful." *Alternative spellings:* Geffrey, Godfrey, Gottfried, Jefferies, Jefferson, Jeffrey, Jeffries, Jefry. *Short forms:* Geoff, Jeff, Jeffy.

George:
From the Greek meaning "farmer."
Alternative spellings: Egor, Georg, Georges, Georgi, Georgie, Goran, Igor, Jorge, Jorn, Juergen, Jurgen, Yorick, Yuri.

Gerald:
From the Old German meaning "spear brave," "spear strong," or "warrior." *Alternative spelling:* Jerald. *Short forms:* Gerry, Jerry.

Gerard:
From the Old German meaning "spear hard" or "rules by the spear." *Alternative spellings:* Gearard, Geraint, Gerardo, Gerhard, Gerrard, Jerrald, Jerrold. *Short forms:* Garry, Gerry, Jerry.

Gerardo:
The Spanish form of Gerrard.

Gerlad:
From the Welsh meaning "unknown."

Germaine:
See Jermaine.

German:
See Germaine.

Gerry:
See Gerald or Gerard.

Giancarlo:
A blend of the Italian names Gian and Carlo.

Gianni:
Familiar form of Giovanni, equivalent of Johnny.

Gideon:
From the Hebrew meaning "cutter," "one who cuts down."

Gilbert:
From the Old German meaning "bright lad" or "a famous or bright pledge." *Short forms:* Bert, Bertie, Burt, Gil.

Gilberto:
The Spanish form of Gilbert.

Giles:
From the Greek meaning "young shield," "cripple," "kid goat," or "goat skin."

Giovanni:
The Italian form of John. *Alternative spellings:* Giovani, Giovanny.

Glenn:
From the Welsh meaning "from the valley." *Alternative spellings:* Glen, Glennard, Glyn, Glynn.

G

Gonzalo:
From the Spanish meaning "wolf" or possibly the German meaning "saved from battle."

Gordon:
From the Old English or Scottish meaning "from the marshes" or "small wooded dell marsh."

Grady:
From the Irish meaning "noble, Illustrious."

Graham:
From the Scottish meaning "farm home"; the Greek meaning "old"; or the Latin meaning "grain."

Grant:
From the English or Scottish meaning "bestow," "great," or "tall" or the Old French *granter,* meaning "to agree."

Grayson:
From the English meaning "son of the bailiff." *Alternative spelling:* Greyson.

Gregory:
From the Greek meaning "watchman." *Alternative spellings:* Greggory, Gregor, Gregori, Gregorio, Grigor. *Short forms:* Greg, Gregg.

Griffin:
From the Welsh meaning "fighting chief" or "fierce" or possibly from the Welsh name Gruffydd, meaning "lord." *Alternative spellings:* Griffen, Gryphon. *Short form:* Griff.

Guillermo:
The Spanish form of William.

Gunnar:
The Scandinavian form of Gunther. *Alternative spelling:* Gunner.

Gunther:
From the German meaning "battler, warrior."

Gustave:
From the Scandinavian meaning "staff of the Goths."

Gustavo:
The Italian form of Gustave.

Guy:
From the Welsh meaning "lively" or the German meaning "wood" or "wide." *Alternative spelling:* Guido.

Gwayne:
From the Welsh meaning "white hawk."

H

Hadrian:
See Adrian.

Hamilton:
From the Old English meaning "proud estate" or "scarred and crooked hill."

Hamza:
From the Arabic meaning "powerful, lion."

Hardy:
From the German meaning "bold, brave."

Harley:
From the Middle Low German meaning "hemp field."

Harold:
From the Old Norse meaning "army power," "leader," or "commander of an army" or the Old German meaning "leader of an army."

Harper:
From the English meaning "harp player."

Harrison:
From the Old English meaning "son of Harry."

Harry:
See Henry.

Harvey:
From the French meaning "battleworthy."

Hassan:
From the Arabic meaning "handsome" or "good." *Alternative spellings:* Hasan, Hussain, Hussein.

Hayden:
From the Old English meaning "pasture land." *Alternative spellings:* Haden, Haiden, Haydn.

Heath:
From the Old English meaning "the heathland dweller."

Hector:
From the Greek meaning "hold fast" or "anchor."

Henry:
From the Old German meaning "ruler of the house." *Alternative spellings:* Enrico, Enrique, Enzio, Ezio, Hedrick, Heindrick, Heinrich, Heinrick, Heinrik, Heinz, Hendrick, Henny, Henri, Henric, Henrik. *Short forms:* Hal, Hank, Harry, Rick, Rik.

Herbert:
From the Old German meaning "bright army."

H

Hezekiah:
From the Hebrew meaning "God gives strength."

Hiram:
From the Hebrew meaning "noble brother."

Holden:
From the English meaning "sheltered place" or "one who keeps watch."

Homer:
From the Greek meaning "being hostage/led" or "blind man."

Horatio:
From the Latin meaning "punctual."
Alternative spellings: Horacio, Horatius.

Hosea:
From the Hebrew meaning "salvation."

Houston:
From the Gaelic and Old English meaning "Hugh's town" or "settlement on the hill." A city in Texas.

Howard:
Possibly from the Old English meaning "hog warden" or "guardian of an enclosure."

Hubert:
From the Old German meaning "bright mind."

Hudson:
From the Old English meaning "son of Hugh."

Hugh:
From the Old German meaning "bright mind," "intelligent," or "noble spirited."
Alternative spellings: Hew, Huw.

Hugo:
The Spanish form of Hugh.

Humbert:
From the Old German meaning "famous giant or renowned warrior."

Humberto:
The Spanish form of Humbert.

Humphrey:
From the Old English meaning "giant peace" or the Old German meaning "strength of peace."

Hunter:
From the English meaning "one who hunts."

Iago:

From the Spanish and Welsh. A variant of James.

Ian:

The Scottish form of John; see also Ieuan. *Alternative spellings:* Iain, Ifan, Iwan, Eion, Ewan.

Ibrahim:

The Arabic form of Abraham.

Ido:

From the Hebrew and Arabic origin, meaning "evaporate" or "to be mighty."

Igor:

The Russian form of George.

Immanuel:

The German form of Emanuel.

Idris:

From the Welsh, meaning "eager lord."

Ira:

From the Hebrew meaning "watchful."

Iestyn:

See Justin.

Irvin:

From the Scottish place name, or from the Gaelic meaning "fair" or "handsome." *Alternative spellings:* Irvine, Irving.

Ieuan:

The Welsh form of John. *Alternative spellings:* Ian, Iain, Ifan, Iwan, Ewan.

Irwin:

From the Old English meaning "boar" and "friend."

Ignacio:

The Spanish and Italian form of Ignatius.

Ignatius:

From the Greek meaning "fire." *Alternative spellings:* Ignacius, Ignatz, Ignazio, Inigo. *Short form:* Iggy.

Isaac:

From the Hebrew meaning "laughter." *Alternative spellings:* Issac, Izaak. *Short forms:* Ike, Zak.

Isai:
Short form of Isaiah.

Isaiah:
From the Hebrew meaning "salvation of the Lord." *Alternative spellings:* Isaias, Isiah, Izaiah, Izayah. *Short forms:* Isa, Izzie.

Isaias:
See Isaiah.

Ishmael:
From the Hebrew meaning "God hears" or "outcast." *Alternative spelling:* Ismael.

Isiah:
See Isaiah.

Isidore:
From the Greek meaning "gift of Isis."

Ismael:
The Spanish form of Ishmael.

Israel:
From the Hebrew meaning "he who strives with God" or "may God prevail."

Issac:
See Isaac.

Istvan:
See Stephen.

Ivan:
The Belorussian or Ukranian version of John. *Short forms:* Ivo, Van.

Ivo:
From the German meaning "yew wood" or "bow wood"; see also Ivan. *Alternative spelling:* Yves.

Ivor:
From the Old Norse meaning "bow" and *herr,* meaning "warrior"; the Welsh meaning "Lord"; or the Latin word *ibor,* meaning "ivory."

Izaiah:
See Isaiah.

Izayah:
See Isaiah.

J

Jabari:
From the Swahili meaning "comforter, consoler."

Jace:
A short form of Jason. A contemporary blend of J and C. *Alternative spellings:* Jase, Jayce.

Jack:
See John.

Jackson:
From the Old English meaning "son of Jack."

Jacob:
From the Hebrew meaning "deceiver" or "supplanter." *Alternative spellings:* Jacques, Jago, Jakob, James, Yakov. *Short forms:* Jake, Jackie.

Jacoby:
A form of Jacob.

Jagger:
From the English meaning "carter."

Jaime:
The Spanish form of Jacob, James.

Jair:
A form of Jairo.

Jairo:
From the Spanish "God enlightens."

Jake:
See Jacob.

Jalen:
See Jaylen.

Jamal:
From the Arabic meaning "handsome." *Alternative spellings:* Jamel, Jamil.

Jamar:
A contemporary invented name based on Jamal. *Alternative spellings:* Jamari, Jamarion, Jamel, Jamir.

Jamarcus:
A contemporary invented name. A blend of Ja and Marcus.

James:
From the Hebrew meaning "supplanter." *Alternative spellings:* Diego, Hamish, Jago, Seamus. *Short forms:* Jamie, Jaime, Jim, Jimbo, Jimmie, Jimmy.

Jameson:
From the English or Celtic meaning "son of James." *Alternative spelling:* Jamison.

Jamie:
See James.

Jaquan:
A contemporary invented name.

Jared:
From the Hebrew meaning "descent" or "descending." *Alternative spelling:* Jarod.

Jaron:
From the Hebrew meaning "to sing out." *Alternative spelling:* Jaren.

Jarrett:
Variant of the surname Garrett (Old English), meaning "spear-brave." Alternative spelling: Jarret.

Jarvis:
French variant of Gervaise, meaning "spearman."

Jasiah:
A contemporary invented name. A blend of Jason and Isiah.

Jason:
From the Greek meaning "healer" or "to heal." *Alternative spelling:* Jayson. *Short forms:* Jay, Jayce.

Jasper:
From the Persian meaning "treasure holder" or the French meaning "green ornamental stone." *Alternative spellings:* Caspar, Casper, Gaspar, Kaspa.

Javan:
From the Hebrew meaning "son of Japheth." *Alternative spellings:* Javen, Javion, Javon, Jayvion, Jayvon.

Javier:
From the Spanish or Portuguese meaning "bright." *Alternative spelling:* Xavier.

Javon:
A form of Javan. *Alternative spellings:* Jayvion, Jayvon.

Jax:
A contemporary invented name. Short form of Jaxon.

Jaxon:
A form of Jackson. *Alternative spelling:* Jackson.

Jay:
Short form of most names beginning with J, now a name in its own right; also from the Latin *gaius,* meaning "jay," as in the bird.

Jayden:

From the Hebrew meaning "God has heard." *Alternative spellings:* Jaden, Jadon, Jaydan, Jaydin, Jaydon.

Jaylen:

A contemporary invented name. A blend of Jay and Len. *Alternative spellings:* Jaylan, Jaylin, Jaylon.

Jean:

See John.

Jed:

From the Hebrew meaning "friend of the Lord" or the Arabic *yed,* meaning "hand."

Jedidiah:

From the Hebrew meaning "Beloved of Jehovah." *Short form:* Jed.

Jefferson:

From the English meaning "son of Jeffrey."

Jeffrey:

See Geoffrey. *Alternative spellings:* Jeffery, Jeffory. *Short form:* Jeff

Jerald:

See Gerald.

Jeremiah:

From the Hebrew meaning "God exalts," "God is on high." *Short forms:* Jeremy, Jerry.

Jeremy:

See Jeremiah. *Short forms:* Jem, Jerry.

Jermaine:

From the Latin meaning "brotherly." *Alternative spellings:* Germaine.

Jerome:

From the Greek name Hieronymus, meaning "holy name."

Jerry:

Familiar form of Gerald or Jerome.

Jesse:

From the Hebrew meaning "God exists," "gift," or "wealthy one." *Alternative spelling:* Jessie.

Jessie:

A form of Jesse.

Jesus:

From the Aramaic meaning "Savior" or "God is salvation." *Alternative spellings:* Husus, Jesuso. *Short form:* Jesu.

J

J

Jethro:
From the Hebrew meaning "abundance" or "overflowing."

Jett:
From the hard, black mineral.

Jimmy:
Familiar form of James.

Joachim:
From the Hebrew meaning "established by God." *Alternative spellings:* Achim, Joaquin, Yackim.

Joan:
A form of John.

Joaquin:
See Joachim.

Jody:
From the Hebrew meaning "persecuted," "hated," or "oppressed."

Joe:
See Joseph.

Joel:
From the Hebrew meaning "Jehovah is God" or "God is willing."

Joey:
Familiar form of Joseph.

Johan:
The German form of John.

John:
From the Hebrew meaning "God is gracious." *Alternative spellings:* Eoin, Euan, Evan, Ewan, Ewen, Giovanni, Hans, Ian, Ivan, Iwan, Iwen, Jack, Jago, Jan, Janos, Jay, Jean, Job, Jon, Juan, Sean, Shane, Shaun, Shawn, Zane, Zain.

Jonah:
From the Hebrew meaning "dove."

Jonas:
The Greek form of Jonah.

Jonathan:
From the Hebrew meaning "God has given." *Alternative spellings:* Johnathon, Jonathon, Jonothan. *Short forms:* Jay, Jon, John, Johnny.

Jordan:
From the Hebrew meaning "flowing down." *Alternative spellings:* Jorden, Jordon, Jordyn.

Jorge:
The Spanish form of George.

José:
The Spanish form of Joseph.

Joseph:
From the Hebrew meaning "God shall add." *Alternative spellings:* Josef, Josephe, Joszef, Yusef. *Short forms:* Beppe, Beppi, Che, Chepe, Jodey, Jody, Joe, Joey, Pepe, Pepito, Pipo.

Joshua:
From the hebrew, meaning "Jehova saves." *Alternative spellings:* Joshuah, Joushua, Jozua. *Short forms:* Josh.

Josiah:
From the Hebrew meaning "fire of the Lord."

Josue:
A form of Joshua.

Jovan:
From the Latin meaning "Jove like, majestic." *Alternative spellings:* Jovani, Jovanni, Jovanny, Jovany.

Juan:
The Spanish form of John.

Judah:
From the Hebrew meaning "praised." *Short form:* Jude.

Jude:
See Judah.

Julian:
From the Greek, meaning "Jove's child." *Alternative spelling:* Julien. *Short forms:* Jules.

Julio:
The Spanish form of Julius.

Julius:
From the Latin meaning "youthful."

Junior:
From the Latin meaning "young."

Justice:
From the Latin meaning "righteous, just, fair." *Alternative spelling:* Justus.

Justin
From Latin origin, meaning "just, upright, righteous." Alternative spelling: Justyn *Short forms:* Jules.

Justus:
A form of Justice.

K

Kade:
See Cade.

Kaden:
See Caden. *Alternative spellings:* Kadin, Kadyn, Kaeden, Kaiden.

Kai:
From the Hawaiian meaning "sea."

Kale:
See Cale.

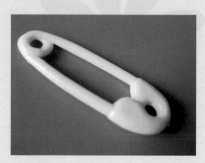

Kaleb:
See Caleb.

Kamal:
From the Arabic, meaning "perfection, perfect."

Kamari:
From the Swahili meaning "moonlight."

Kamden:
See Camden.

Kameron:
See Cameron. *Alternative forms:* Kamron, Kamryn.

Kane:
From the Irish Gaelic meaning "son of Cathan" or the Hebrew meaning "a spear" or "spear gatherer." *Alternative forms:* Cahan, Cain.

Kareem:
From the Arabic meaning "noble, distinguished."

Karl:
See Carl.

Karson:
See Carson.

Karter:
See Carter.

Kasey:
See Casey.

Kason:
A contemporary invented name. Jason with a K. *Alternative spelling:* Kasen.

Kaspar:
See Jasper or Casper. *Alternative spellings:* Casper, Jaspar, Jasper, Kaspa, Kasper.

Kayden:
See Caden.

Keane:
From the Irish, meaning "fighter; sharp, keen wit."

Keanu:
From the Hawaiian, meaning "the breeze."

Keaton:
From the English meaning "where the hawks fly."

Keegan:
From the Irish meaning "little fiery one." *Alternative spelling:* Keagan.

Keelin:
From the Gaelic meaning "slender" and "white" or possibly from the Irish Gaelic meaning "mighty warrior." *Alternative spellings:* Keely, Kellen.

Keenan:
From the Irish meaning "ancient."

Keir:
From the Gaelic meaning "of dark complexion."

Keith:
From the Gaelic meaning "wood" or "windy place."

Kellen:
From the Irish meaning "mighty warrior." *Alternative spellings:* Kelan, Kellan.

Kelsey:
From the Old English *ceol,* meaning "ship," and *sige,* meaning "victory."

Kelton:
From the English meaning "keel town or port."

Kelvin:
Possibly from the Old English meaning "water's friend" or the Scottish Gaelic meaning "from the narrow stream."

K

Kendall:
From the Celtic meaning "ruler of the valley."

Kendrick:
From the English and Scottish meaning "royal ruler, chieftain."

Kenneth:
From the Gaelic meaning "handsome." *Short form:* Kenny.

Kenyon:
From the English or Irish meaning "white haired or blond."

Keon:
A contemporary form of Ewan. *Alternative spellings:* Keyon, Kian.

Keshawn:
Of contemporary origin. An invented name combining Ke and Shawn. *Alternative spelling:* Keshaun.

Kevin:
From the Gaelic *caoimhín,* meaning "beloved." *Alternative spellings:* Kevan, Keven.

Keyon:
See Keon.

Khalid:
From the Arabic, meaning "immortal, eternal." *Alternative spelling:* Khaled.

Khalil:
From the Arabic meaning "friend."

Kian:
See Keon.

Kieran:
From the Irish meaning "little dark one." *Alternative spellings:* Cieran, Cieron, Kieron. *Short form:* Kier.

Kiernan:
Derived from the Irish *ciar,* meaning "black." *Alternative spelling:* Kearnan.

Killian:
From the Irish meaning "war, strife, or church." *Alternative spelling:* Kilian.

Kim:
From the Old English meaning "royally born."

King:
From the English meaning "Monarch."

Kingston:
From the English meaning "Kings estate."

Kirk:
From the Old Norse meaning "church."

Kobe:
From the Swahili meaning "tortoise."

Kody:
See Cody.

Kofi:
From the Ghanaian, meaning "born on Friday."

Kolby:
See Colby.

Kole:
See Cole.

Kolton:
See Colton.

Konner:
See Connor. *Alternative spelling:* Konnor.

Konnor:
See Connor.

Korbin:
See Corbin.

Krish:
From the Sanskrit meaning "dark, black." A short form of Krishna.

Kristian:
The Danish and Greek form of Christian.

Kristofer:
See Christopher. *Short form:* Kris.

Kristopher:
The Greek form of Christopher.

Kurt:
See Curtis.

Kylan:
Of contemporary origin. An invented name combining Kyle and Dylan.

Kyle:
From the Gaelic *caol*, meaning "narrow."

Kyler:
From the Dutch meaning "bowman, archer."

L

Lachlan:
From the Scottish Gaelic meaning "fjord land" or "land of the lakes." *Short forms:* Lachie, Lochie.

Lamar:
From the German meaning "famous throughout the land" or the French meaning "sea" or "ocean."

Lamont:
From the Scandinavian meaning "lawyer." *Alternative spellings:* Lammond, Lamond, Lamonte.

Lance:
From the Old German meaning "land"; see also Lancelot. *Alternative spelling:* Launce.

Lancelot:
From the Latin meaning "lance" or the French meaning "attendant." *Alternative spelling:* Launcelot. *Short forms:* Lance, Launce.

Lando:
Short form of Orlando.

Landon:
From the English meaning "grassy plain." *Alternative spellings:* Landen, Landin, Landyn.

Lane:
From the English meaning "narrow road or path." *Alternative spelling:* Layne.

Larry:
See Lawrence.

Lars:
See Lawrence.

Larsen:
See Lawrence.

Larson:
See Lawrence. *Alternative spelling:* Larsen.

Laszlo:
From the Hungarian meaning "famous ruler." *Alternative spellings:* Laslo, Lazlo.

Lawrence:
From the Latin *lawrentium,* meaning "the place of the laurel trees" or "laurel crowned." *Alternative spellings:* Larsen, Larson, Laurencio, Laurens, Laurence, Laurent, Lorenzo. *Short forms:* Lars, Larry, Larrie, Lauren, Laurie, Lorn, Lorne.

Lawson:
From the English meaning "son of Lawrence."

Layton:
From the English meaning "meadow settlement." *Alternative spelling:* Leighton.

Leander:
From the Greek meaning "brave as a lion" or "lion man." *Alternative spelling:* Leandro. *Short forms:* Lea, Lee, Leo.

Leandro:
The Spanish form of Leander

Lee:
From the Old English meaning "meadow"; see also Leander. *Alternative spelling:* Leigh.

Leif:
From the Scandinavian meaning "beloved" or possibly "son" or "descendant." *Alternative spelling:* Llef.

Leigh:
See Lee.

Leks:
See Alexander.

Leland:
From the Old English meaning "fallow land."

Lennart:
See Leonard.

Lennon:
From the Gaelic Irish meaning "small cloak" or "cape."

Lennox:
From the Gaelic Scottish meaning "with many elms." *Alternative spelling:* Lenox.

Leo:
From the Latin meaning "lion"; see also Leonard or Leopold. *Alternative spelling:* Lev.

Leolin:
From the Welsh meaning "lionlike."

Leon:
From the Latin meaning "lion."

Leonard:
From the Old German meaning "as strong as a lion." *Alternative spellings:* Lennaert, Lennard, Lennart, Leonardo, Leonart, Leonidas, Leonides. *Short form:* Len, Lenny, Leo.

Leonardo:
The Spanish and Italian form of Leonard.

L

Leonel:
See Lionel.

Leopold:
From the Old German meaning "brave people." *Alternative spelling:* Leopoldo. *Short form:* Leo.

Leroy:
From the Old French meaning "the king."

Leslie:
From the Scottish place name or from the Scottish Gaelic meaning "gray fortress." *Alternative spelling:* Leslee. *Short forms:* Lee, Les.

Lester:
From the Latin meaning "chosen camp" or from the English city Leicester. *Short form:* Les.

Lestyn:
Welsh derivative from the Latin word for "just."

Lev:
From the Hebrew meaning "heart" or the Russian form of Leo.

Levi:
From the Hebrew, meaning "joined."

Lewis:
See Louis, possibly also from the Celtic meaning "lionlike." *Short form:* Lew.

Lex:
See Alexander.

Liam:
The Irish form of William.

Lincoln:
From the English meaning "town by the pool."

Lindon:
See Lyndon.

Lindsay:
From the Scottish family name of the Earls of Crawford or possibly from the Old English meaning "linden tree island." *Alternative spellings:* Lindsey, Linsey, Linsay.

Linford:
From the Old English meaning "linden-tree ford" or "flax river crossing." *Alternative spelling:* Lynford.

Linley:
From the Old English meaning "flax meadow."

Linus:
From the Greek meaning "flaxen-haired" or "net."

Lionel:
From the Latin meaning "little lion" or "lion cub." *Alternative spelling:* Leonel.

Llew:
From the Welsh meaning "lion."

Lloyd:
From the Welsh meaning "gray." *Alternative spelling:* Floyd.

Llyr:
From Welsh, originating from the ancient sea god Lear.

Logan:
From the Scottish meaning "low meadow" or possibly from the Scottish place of the same name in Ayrshire.

Lon:
See Alphonse.

London:
From the English meaning "fortress of the moon." The capital city of the United Kingdom.

Lonnie:
See Alphonse.

Lorcan:
From the Irish meaning "little" or "fierce."

Lorenzo:
The Italian form of Lawrence.

Lorne:
See Lawrence. *Alternative spelling:* Lorn.

Lothar:
From the German, meaning "famous warrior."

Lother:
See Luther.

Lou:
See Louis.

Louie:
See Louis.

Louis:
From the German meaning "famous warrior" or the French meaning "famous." *Alternative spellings:* Lewis, Ludovic, Ludwig, Luigi, Luis, Lutek. *Short forms:* Lou, Louie.

L

Lovell:
From the French meaning "wolf cub."

Luca:
The Italian form of Lucius.

Lucas:
From the Latin meaning "light" or "bringer of light" or possibly from the Latin meaning "man from Lucania," a place in Southern Italy. *Alternative spellings:* Luckas, Lucius, Lucus, Lukas. *Short form:* Luc, Luke.

Lucian:
See Lucius.

Luciano:
The Italian form of Lucian.

Lucien:
See Lucius.

Lucius:
See Lucas. *Alternative spellings:* Lucian, Lucien, Lucio. *Short forms:* Luc, Luca, Luka, Lukas, Luke.

Luigi:
The Italian form of Louis.

Luis:
The French and German form of Louis.

Luka:
The Italian form of Luke.

Lukas:
The German form of Lucas.

Luke:
From the Greek *loukas,* meaning "man from Lucania"; see also Lucius or Lucas.

Luther:
From the Old German meaning "famous warrior." *Alternative spellings:* Lothar, Lother, Luthor.

Lyall:
From the Norse, meaning "wolf."

Lyndon:
From the Old English meaning "linden-tree hill." *Alternative spelling:* Lindon.

M

Madden:
From the Irish meaning "little Dog."

Maddock:
From the Welsh meaning "generous."
Alternative spellings: Madoc, Madock, Madog.

Maddox:
From the Welsh meaning "benefactor's son."

Madison:
From the English meaning "son of Maud" or "good son." *Alternative spellings:* Maddie, Maddison, Maddy, Madisson.

Magnus:
From the Latin meaning "great."

Makai:
The Hawaiian form of Matthew.
Alternative spelling: Makaio.

Malachi:
From the Hebrew meaning "messenger."
Alternative spellings: Malakai, Malaki.

Malcolm:
From the Gaelic *maol, Caluim* meaning "servant of Columba." *Alternative spellings:* Calum, Callum, Kalum, Kallum, Malcom, Malkolm. *Short form:* Mal.

Malik:
From the Hebrew meaning "reigning" or the Punjabi meaning "lord" or "master."

Manuel:
See Emanuel.

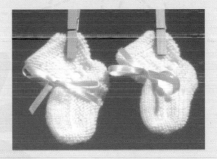

Marc:
See Marcus. *Alternative spelling:* Mark.

Marcel:
See Marcus. *Alternative spellings:* Marcelo, Marchello, Marsello, Marselo.

Marco:
The Italian form of Mark.

Marcus:
From the Roman god of war, Mars.
Alternative spellings: Marcel, Marcellus, Marcio, Marco, Marcos, Marek, Marius, Mark, Marko, Markov, Markus.
Short forms: Marc, Mark.

M

Marian:
See Mark.

Mariano:
An Italian form of Mark.

Mario:
The Italian form of Marius.

Marius:
Possibly from Mars, the Roman god of war or the adjective "mas," meaning "male, manly."

Mark:
See Marcus.

Markus:
See Marcus.

Marlon:
From the English meaning "little hawk." Possibly a variant of Merlin.

Marques:
The Spanish or Portuguese form of Marquis.

Marquis:
From the French meaning "Lord of the marches; noble rank." An English rank of nobleman. *Alternative spelling:* Marquise.

Marshall:
From the French meaning "one who looks after horses."

Martin:
From the Latin meaning "martial, warlike."

Marvin:
From the English meaning "lover of the sea."

Mason:
From a surname meaning "stoneworker" in Old French, ultimately derived from Germanic and akin to Old English *macian,* meaning "to make."

Mathias:
See Matthew. *Alternative spellings:* Matthais, Mathis, Matteus.

Matteo:
The Spanish form of Matthew.

Matthew:
From the Hebrew meaning "gift of the Lord." *Alternative spellings:* Maitia, Mateo, Matheu, Mathew, Mathias, Mathieu, Mathiew, Mathis, Mattek, Matthaus. Mattheus, Matthieu, Mattia, Mattias, Mattieux. *Short forms:* Mat, Mati, Matie, Matt, Mattie, Matty, Maty.

Maurice:

From the Latin meaning "dark-skinned" or the Greek meaning "Moor." *Alternative spellings:* Maruin, Mauricio, Maurio, Mauritz, Maury, Morice, Moris, Morrice, Morris.

Mauricio:

The Spanish form of Maurice.

Maverick:

Of American origin, meaning "an independent man who avoids conformity."

Max:

See Maximillian or Maxwell.

Maxime:

From the French meaning "most excellent." *Alternative spelling:* Maxim.

Maximillian:

From the Latin meaning "greatest." *Alternative spellings:* Massimilliano, Maxim, Maximilien, Maximilion, Maximo, Maximos. *Short forms:* Max, Maxie, Maxy, Milo.

Maximo:

The Spanish form of Maximus.

Maximus:

From the Latin for "the greatest."

Maxwell:

From the English meaning "great spring" or possibly the Scottish Gaelic meaning "Mack's well." *Short forms:* Max, Maxie, Maxy.

Maynard:

From the English meaning "powerful."

Mekhi:

A contemporary invented name. Possibly a form of Meka from the Hawaiian meaning "eyes."

Melvin:

From the Celtic meaning "chief" or the Gaelic meaning "smooth brow." *Alternative spellings:* Melvino, Melvyn. *Short form:* Mel.

Memphis:

From the Egyptian meaning "one who comes from Memphis." A town in Tennessee.

Meredith:

From the Welsh meaning "guardian of the sea" or "great chief." *Alternative spellings:* Meredyth, Merideth, Meridith. *Short form:* Merry.

M

Merion:
From the Welsh place Merion; see also Merlin.

Merle:
See Merlin or Merill; possibly also from the French meaning "blackbird."

Merlin:
From the Welsh name Myrddin, meaning "sea fort." *Alternative spellings:* Marlon, Merion, Merle, Merlen, Merlinn, Merlyn.

Merrick:
From the English meaning "ruler of the sea." *Alternative spellings:* Mayrick, Merek, Meric, Merrik.

Merrill:
From the Irish meaning "bright sea" or the French meaning "famous." *Alternative spellings:* Meril, Merill, Merle, Merrel, Merrell, Merril, Meryl.

Mervin:
From the Welsh Myrddin meaning "sea hill." *Alternative spelling:* Mervyn. *Short form:* Merv.

Messiah:
From the Hebrew meaning "the anointed One."

Micah:
From the Hebrew meaning "who is like Yahweh [God]." *Alternative spellings:* Mica, Micaiah, Mikah.

Michael:
The Greek form of Micah. *Alternative spellings:* Michaele, Michail, Michal, Michale, Michel, Michele, Michelet, Mikael, Mitchell. *Short forms:* Mic, Mick, Micky, Miguel, Mihail, Mik, Mike, Mikey, Miki, Mikie, Mikki, Misha.

Miguel:
The Spanish form of Michael.

Miles:
From the Old German meaning "gentle" or possibly "generous" or "merciful"; the Latin meaning "soldier"; or the Greek meaning "millstone." *Alternative spelling:* Myles.

Milo:
The Spanish form of Miles.

Milton:
From the English meaning "mill town."

Misael:
The Hebrew form of Michael.

Mishka:
From the Russian meaning "little bear."

Mitch:
See Mitchell.

Mitchell:
From the Middle English meaning "who is like God"; see also Michael. *Short form:* Mitch.

Mohammed:
From the Arabic meaning "praised." *Alternative spellings:* Mohamad, Mohamed, Mohamet, Mohammad, Mohammed, Muhammed. *Short forms:* Ahmad, Ahmet, Amad, Amed, Hamad, Hamid, Hammed, Mehmet.

Moises:
The Spanish form of Moses.

Monroe:
From the Scottish meaning "from the river's mouth" or "wheel turner." *Alternative spellings:* Monro, Munro, Munroe.

Montgomery:
From the English meaning "rich man's mountain" or "mountain of one who rules." *Short form:* Monty.

Moray:
From the Celtic meaning "sea." *Alternative spelling:* Murray.

Mordechai:
From the Hebrew meaning "martial" or "warlike." *Alternative spellings:* Mordecai. *Short forms:* Mort, Morty.

Mordred:
From the Latin meaning "painful."

Morgan:
From the Welsh meaning "sea dweller" or "great" and "bright." *Alternative spellings:* Morcant, Morgen.

Moses:
From the Hebrew meaning "delivered" or the Egyptian meaning "child" or "son." *Alternative spellings:* Moise, Moises, Moishe, Moyses. *Short forms:* Mo, Moe, Moss.

Moshe:
The Hebrew form of Moses.

Muhammad:
See Mohammed.

Myles:
See Miles.

N

Nash:
From the English meaning "by the ash tree."

Nasir:
See Nasser.

Nasser:
From the Arabic meaning "victorious." *Alternative spelling:* Nasir.

Nathan:
From the Hebrew meaning "gift." *Short forms:* Nat, Nate, Natal.

Nathaniel:
From the Hebrew meaning "gift of God." *Alternative spellings:* Nathanael, Nathanial. *Short forms:* Nat, Nathan.

Nehemiah:
From the Hebrew meaning "the Lord's comfort."

Neil:
From the Irish Gaelic *niadh,* meaning "champion" or possibly from the Old Norse name Niel. *Alternative spellings:* Neal, Neale, Neill, Neils, Niall, Niel, Niels, Niles, Nils, Nilson.

Nelson:
From the English meaning "Neil's son."

Nery:
From the Hebrew name Nuri, meaning "my life."

Nestor:
From the Greek meaning "traveler," "remember," or "wise."

Niall:
See Neil.

Nicholas:
From the Greek meaning "victory of the people." *Alternative spellings:* Nicolas, Nikolai, Nikolas, Nikolaus, Nikolos. *Short forms:* Claus, Colin, Klaus, Nic, Nick, Nickie, Nicky, Nico, Nicol, Nicolai, Nicoll, Nik, Niki, Nikki, Niko, Nilo.

Nick:
See Nicholas.

Nico:
Short form for all names beginning Nico-. *Alternative spelling:* Niko.

Nigel:
From the Irish Gaelic meaning "champion"; the Latin *nigellus,* meaning "black" or "dark" or the Old English meaning "night." *Short form:* Nige.

Nikhil:
From the Sanskrit meaning "entire, all."

Niles:
See Neil.

Noah:
From the Hebrew meaning "rest." *Alternative spelling: Noach.*

Noe:
See Noah.

Noel:
From the French meaning "Christ's birthday," "Christmas."

Nolan:
From the Celtic meaning "famous" or "noble" or possibly from the Irish meaning "shout." *Alternative spelling: Nolen.*

Norman:
From the Old English meaning "man from the North."

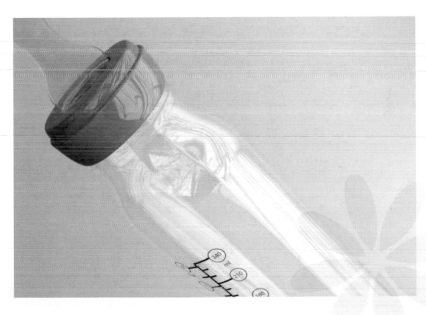

O

Obadiah:
From the Hebrew, meaning "servant of God."

Oberon:
From the German meaning "noble" or "bearlike."

Octavio:
From the Latin meaning "eighth."
Alternative spelling: Octave.

Odell:
From the Greek meaning "ode" or "melody"; the Irish meaning "otter"; or the English meaning "forested hill."

Odin:
From the Norse. Odin was the chief god of Norse mythology.

Odo:
From the Old English *ead,* meaning "rich."

Ogden:
From the Old English meaning "oak tree valley."

Olav:
From the Old Norse meaning "ancestor."
Alternative spelling: Olaf.

Oleg:
From the Russian meaning "holy."

Oliver:
From the French meaning "olive tree."
Alternative spellings: Olivier, Oliviero.
Short forms: Oli, Olli, Olly.

Omar:
From the Arabic meaning "eloquent," "highest," or "long life."

Omari:
The Swahili form of Omar.

Omarion:
A variation of Omari.

Oran:
From the Irish Gaelic meaning "green."

Oren:
From the Hebrew meaning "pine tree."

Orion:
From the Greek meaning "son of fire."

Orlando:
From the German or Spanish meaning "famous throughout the land"; see also Roland. *Alternative spellings:* Olando, Orland, Orlanda, Orlandus, Orlondo.
Short forms: Lando, Olo, Orlan, Orlo.

Orrin:
From the English. The name of a river in England.

Orson:
From the Latin meaning "bear."

Orville:
From the French meaning "gold town."

Oscar:
From the Old English meaning "divine spear." *Alternative spelling: Oskar.*

Osmond:
From the Old English meaning "protected by God." *Alternative spellings: Åsmund, Osmand, Osmund, Osmundo. Short forms:* Os, Ossie, Oz, Ozzie.

Osvaldo:
The Spanish form of Oswald. *Alternative spelling: Oswaldo.*

Oswald:
From the Old English meaning "divine power." *Alternative spellings: Osvaldo, Oswaldo, Oswold. Short forms:* Os, Ossie, Oz, Ozzie.

Otis:
From the Greek meaning "keen of hearing."

Otto:
From the Old German meaning "possessions."

Owen:
Anglicized form of Eoghan.

P–Q

Pablo:
See Paul.

Paddy:
See Patrick.

Paine:
From the Latin, meaning "countryman, rustic villager, peasant."

Paolo:
See Paul.

Parker:
From the English meaning "park keeper."

Pascal:
From the French meaning "Easter." *Alternative spellings:* Pascoe, Pascual, Pasqual, Pasquale.

Patrick:
From the Latin meaning "noble." *Alternative spellings:* Padraig, Padriac, Padrig, Patric, Patrice, Patricio, Peyton. *Short forms:* Paddy, Pat, Patsy.

Paul:
From the Latin meaning "small." *Alternative spellings:* Pablo, Paolo, Paulo, Pavel.

Paxton:
From the Latin meaning "peaceful town."

Pedro:
The Spanish form of Peter.

Percival:
From the French meaning "penetrate the valley." *Alternative spellings:* Parsifal, Perceval. *Short forms:* Perce, Percy.

Peregrine:
From the Latin meaning "traveler" or "foreigner." *Short form:* Perry.

Pericles:
From the Greek origin, meaning "far-famed."

Perseus:
From the Greek. In mythology, the son of Zeus and Danae.

Peter:
From the Greek *petros,* meaning "stone" or "rock." *Alternative spellings:* Ferris, Pedro, Petros, Petter, Pierce, Pierre, Piers, Pieter. *Short form:* Pete.

Peyton:
From the English meaning "warriors town." *Alternative spelling:* Payton.

Phelan:
From the Irish meaning "wolf."

Philip:
From the Greek meaning "fond of horses." *Alternative spellings:* Felipe, Felippe, Filip, Filippo, Philipp, Phillip, Phillipp. *Short forms:* Phil, Pip.

Phineas:
From the Hebrew meaning "oracle."

Phoenix:
From the Greek meaning "dark red." Also mythical bird that rose from the ashes.

Pierce:
From the Middle English form of Peter.

Porter:
From the Latin meaning "gatekeeper."

Pranav:
From the Hindi, meaning "primordial."

Preston:
From the Old English meaning "priest's statement" or "priest's town."

Prince:
From the Latin meaning "to take first place."

Prior:
From the Latin meaning "the first."

Quentin:
From the Latin meaning "fifth" or possibly from the English meaning "Queen's town." *Alternative spellings:* Quenton, Quintin, Quinton. *Short forms:* Quin, Quinn, Quinny.

Quillan:
From the Irish, meaning "cub."

Quincy:
From the French meaning "fifth son's estate." *Alternative spelling:* Quincey. *Short form:* Quince.

Quinlan:
From the Irish meaning "strong" or "well-shaped."

Quinn:
From the Irish meaning "counsel."

Quinton:
See Quentin.

P–Q

R

Rafael:
The Spanish form of Raphael.

Raiden:
From the Japanese meaning "thunder and lightning." The God of thunder in Japanese mythology.

Ralph:
From the Old English meaning "wolf counsel." *Alternative spellings:* Radolphus, Rafe, Ralf, Ralfie, Ralphael, Ralphel, Ralphie, Raoul, Raul, Rolf.

Ramiro:
From the Spanish meaning "great judge."

Ramon:
The Spanish form of Raymond.

Randall:
From the Old English meaning "shield wolf." *Alternative spellings:* Randall, Randol, Randolf, Randolfo, Randolph. *Short forms:* Randy, Dolph.

Randy:
See Randolph.

Raphael:
From the Hebrew meaning "God has healed." *Alternative spellings:* Rafael, Rafaello. *Short forms:* Rafe, Rafi.

Rashad:
From the Arabic meaning "having good judgment."

Raul:
The Spanish form of Ralph.

Ray:
See Raymond.

Raymond:
From the Old English meaning "protector" or "guardian." *Alternative spellings:* Raimond, Raimondo, Ramon, Ramond, Raymund, Redmond. *Short form:* Ray.

Reagan:
From the Irish meaning "descendant of the little king." *Alternative spellings:* Reagen, Regen.

Redmond:
See Raymond.

Reece:
From the Welsh meaning "ardent" or "fiery." *Alternative spellings:* Reese, Rhys.

Reginald:
From the Old German meaning "power force" or "great warrior." *Alternative spellings:* Ranald, Regnault, Reinald, Reinhold, Reinold, Reinwald, Renaldo, Renaud, Renault, Rene, Rex. *Short forms:* Reg, Reggie.

Reid:
From the Old English *read* meaning "red." *Alternative spelling:* Reed.

Reilly:
From the Irish meaning "valiant."

Remington:
From the Old English meaning "ravens town."

Rene:
From the French meaning "reborn."

Reuben:
From the Hebrew meaning "behold a son." *Alternative spellings:* Ruben, Reuven, Rouvin.

Rex:
From the Latin meaning "king"; see also Reginald.

Rey:
See Reynald.

Reynald:
From the English meaning "King's advisor." *Short form:* Rey.

Reynaldo:
The Spanish form of Reynald.

Rhett:
See Rhys.

Rhys:
From the Welsh meaning "ardent" or "fiery." *Alternative spellings:* Reece, Reese, Rhett.

Richard:
From the Old German meaning "strong ruler." *Alternative spellings:* Ricardo, Riccardo, Richardo, Richart. *Short forms:* Dick, Dickie, Dicky, Dixon, Rich, Richie, Rick, Ricky.

Rigoberto:
From the German meaning "splendid, wealthy."

R

Riley:
From the English meaning "rye." *Alternative spellings:* Reilly, Rylee.

Rishi:
From the Sanskrit meaning "sage."

River:
From the English "river."

Robert:
From the English meaning "bright fame." *Alternative spellings:* Roban, Robard, Robin, Rupert. *Short forms:* Bob, Bobbie, Bobby, Rab, Rob, Robbie, Robby.

Roberto:
The Italian and Spanish form of Robert.

Robin:
See Robert. *Alternative spelling:* Robyn.

Rocco:
From the Italian meaning "rock." *Short forms:* Rock, Rocky.

Roderick:
From the Old German meaning "famous ruler." *Alternative spellings:* Roderic, Roderich, Roderigo, Rodrigo, Rodrique, Rurik. *Short forms:* Rod, Rodd, Roddy, Rori, Roric, Rory, Ruy.

Rodney:
From the Old English meaning "reed island." *Short forms:* Rod, Rodd, Roddy.

Rodolfo:
The Spanish form of Rudolph.

Rodrigo:
The Spanish form of Roderick.

Rogelio:
The Spanish form of Roger.

Roger:
From the Old German meaning "famous spear," "renowned warrior." *Alternative spellings:* Rodger, Rudiger, Ruggerio, Rutger, Ruttger.

Rohan:
From the Hindi meaning "sandalwood."

Roland:
From the Old German meaning "famous land." *Alternative spellings:* Rolando, Rollan, Rolland, Rowland, Orlando. *Short form:* Rollo.

Rolando:
The Spanish form of Roland.

Roman:
From the Latin meaning "citizen of Rome."

Romeo:
From the Italian meaning "pilgrim to Rome, Roman."

Ronald:
From the Norse name Rögnvaldr, meaning "decisive ruler." *Alternative spellings:* Ranald, Roald. *Short forms:* Ron, Roni, Ronnie, Ronny.

Ronaldo:
The Spanish form of Ronald.

Ronan:
From the Irish meaning "little seal." *Alternative spelling:* Rowan.

Ronnie:
See Ronald.

Rory:
From Irish and Gaelic origin, meaning "red." A short form of Roderick.

Ross:
From the Gaelic meaning "peninsular."

Rowan:
From the Irish Gaelic meaning "little red one."

Roy:
From the the French meaning "king."

Royce:
From the English meaning "famous."

Ruben:
See Reuben.

Rudolf:
From the Old German meaning "famous wolf." *Alternative spelling:* Rudolph. *Short form:* Rudy.

Rudy:
A familiar form of Rudolf.

Russell:
From the French meaning "redhead, fox colored."

Ryan:
From the Gaelic meaning "king" or "water." *Alternative spellings:* Rian, Ryen.

Ryder:
From the English "rider" meaning "horseman." *Alternative spelling:* Rider.

Ryker:
See Rylan.

Rylan:
From the English and Irish meaning "island meadow." *Alternative spellings:* Ryker, Ryland.

Sage:
From the Latin meaning "wise and knowing."

Salvador:
From the Latin meaning "savior."
Alternative spellings: Salvadore, Salvator, Salvatore.

Sam:
See Samson, Samuel.

Samir:
From the Arabic meaning "entertaining companion."

Samson:
From the Hebrew meaning "child of the sun." *Short form:* Sam.

Samuel:
From the Hebrew meaning "told by God." *Short forms:* Sam, Sammy.

Santiago:
From the Latin meaning "Saint James."

Santino:
See Santo.

Santo:
From the Italian meaning "saint, holy."
Alternative spelling: Santino.

Santos:
From the Spanish meaning "saint, holy."

Sasha:
See Alexander.

Saul:
From the Hebrew meaning "asked for."

Sava:
From the Greek meaning "old man."
Alternative spelling: Savas.

Savion:
A contemporary invented name. Possibly based on Xavier.

Sawyer:
From the English meaning "woodcutter."

Saxon:
From the German meaning "knife."

Sayer:
From Welsh origins, meaning "carpenter."

Scott:
From the Old English meaning "man of Scotland." *Alternative spellings:* Scot, Scottie, Scotty.

Seamus:
See James or Jacob. *Alternative spelling:* Shamus.

Sean:
See John.

Sebastian:
From the Greek meaning "venerable." *Alternative spelling:* Sebastien. *Short forms:* Basti, Bastiano, Bastien, Seb.

Semaj:
A contemporary invented name. James spelled backward.

Sergio:
The Italian form of Serge, from the Latin meaning "attendant, servant."

Seth:
From the Hebrew meaning "appointed."

Seymour:
From the Old English meaning "wild coastal land."

Shamar:
From the Aramaic meaning "a sharp thorn, flint."

Shane:
See John. *Alternative spellings:* Shayne, Sean.

Shannon:
From the Irish Gaelic meaning "wise" or from the name of an Irish river.

Shawn:
See John. *Alternative spellings:* Shaun.

Sheldon:
From the English meaning "farm on the ledge."

Shelly:
From the English meaning "meadow on a slope."

Sidney:
From the Old English meaning "wide, well-watered land" or "meadow by the river." *Alternative spelling:* Sydney. *Short forms:* Sid, Syd.

S

Silas:
From the Greek meaning "wide, well-watered land"; the Hebrew meaning "to borrow"; or the Latin *silus,* meaning "snub-nosed," or *silva,* meaning "wood."

Simon:
From the Greek meaning "snub-nosed" or the Hebrew meaning "he heard." *Alternative spellings:* Shimon, Simeon, Simone. *Short form:* Si.

Sincere:
From the English meaning "honest, genuine."

Skyler:
From the Dutch name Schuyler, meaning "to shelter." *Alternative spelling:* Skylar.

Slade:
From the English meaning "from the valley."

Solomon:
From the Hebrew meaning "peace." *Short forms:* Sol, Solly.

Soren:
From the Danish meaning "thunder, war."

Spencer:
From the Middle English meaning "steward" or "butler."

Stanley:
From the Old English *stan,* meaning "stone," and *leah,* meaning "clearing." *Short form:* Stan.

Stefan:
See Stephen.

Stephen:
From the Greek *stefanos,* meaning "garland," "crown," or "wearer of the crown." *Alternative spellings:* Esteban, Estes, Etienne, Etiennes, Istvan, Stefan, Stefano, Steffan, Stevan, Steven. *Short form:* Steve.

Sterling:
From the English meaning "genuine" and "reliable" or the Old English meaning "star." *Alternative spelling:* Stirling.

Steven:
See Stephen.

Stone:
From the English meaning "stone, rock."

Sullivan:
From the Irish meaning "dark eyes."

T

Talon:
From the French meaning "claw of a bird of prey." *Alternative spellings:* Talan, Talen.

Tanner:
From the English meaning "leather worker."

Tate:
From the Middle English *tayt*, meaning "cheerful" or "spirited."

Taylor:
From the Old English meaning "tailor."

Teagan:
From the Irish meaning "little poet." *Alternative spelling:* Tegan.

Terrance:
From the Latin meaning "tender." *Alternative spellings:* Terance, Terencio, Terrence, Torrance, Torrence. *Short form:* Terry.

Terrell:
From the German meaning "thunder ruler." *Alternative spelling:* Tyrell.

Terry:
See Terrance.

Thaddeus:
See Theodore. *Short form:* Tad, Thad.

Theodore:
From the Greek meaning "God's gift." *Alternative spellings:* Thaddeus, Thadeus, That, Theodor. *Short forms:* Ted, Tedd, Teddie, Teddy, Theo, Todd.

Thomas:
From the Greek *didymos,* meaning "twin." *Alternative spelling:* Tomas. *Short forms:* Tam, Thom, Thoma, Tom, Tommie, Tommy.

Timothy:
From the Greek meaning "honoring God." *Short forms:* Tim, Timmy, Timo.

Titus:
Possibly from the Greek meaning "day" or "sun." *Short form:* Tito.

Tobias:
From the Hebrew meaning "God is good." *Alternative spellings:* Tobin Tobit. *Short forms:* Tobe, Tobey, Tobie, Toby.

Toby:
See Tobias.

Todd:
From the Middle English meaning "fox."

T

Tony:
See Anthony.

Trace:
A contemporary invented name.
Possibly a short form of Tracy.

Tracy:
From the French meaning "of Thracia."

Travis:
From the French meaning "to cross."

Trent:
From the Latin meaning "rapid waters."

Trenton:
From the English meaning "town by the river."

Trevon:
Of contemporary origin. An invented name, a form of Trevor. *Alternative spellings:* Trevion, Treyvon.

Trevor:
From the Welsh meaning "large homestead." *Alternative spelling:* Trefor.

Trey:
From the English meaning "three, third."

Tristan:
From the Celtic meaning "tumult" or "riot." *Alternative spellings:* Tristen, Tristian, Tristin, Triston, Trystan.

Troy:
From the old city in Asia Minor.

Truman:
From the English meaning "true man."

Tucker:
From the English meaning "fabric pleater."

Turner:
From the English meaning "woodworker."

Tyler:
From the Old English meaning "someone who tiles roofs." *Alternative spelling:* Tylor. *Short form:* Ty.

Tyree:
From the Scottish meaning "from Tyrie." *Alternative spelling:* Tyrese.

Tyrone:
From the Irish meaning "Eoghan's land."

Tyson:
From the French meaning "firebrand."

U–V

Ulises:
See Ulysses.

Ulysses:
From the Greek name Odysseus. The meaning is uncertain though it possibly comes from the Latin for "hateful." *Alternative spelling:* Ulises.

Uriah:
From the Hebrew meaning "my light is the Lord." *Alternative spelling:* Uriel.

Uriel:
From the Hebrew meaning "God is my light."

Valentin:
From the Latin *valens,* meaning "to be strong." *Alternative spellings:* Valencio, Valentin, Valentino.

Van:
See Evan or Ivan.

Vance:
From the English meaning "thresher" or "someone who lives near a marsh."

Vaughan:
From the Welsh meaning "little" or "small." *Alternative spelling:* Vaughn.

Vernon:
From the French meaning "alder tree" or "alder grove" or the Latin meaning "springlike" or "youthful." *Short forms:* Vern, Verne.

Vicente:
The Spanish form of Vincent.

Victor:
From the Latin meaning "conqueror." *Alternative spellings:* Victoire, Victorio, Viktor, Vittorio. *Short form:* Vic.

Vincent:
From the Latin meaning "to conquer." *Alternative spellings:* Vicente, Vincenzo. *Short forms:* Vin, Vince, Vinnie, Vinny.

Vincenzo:
The Italian form of Vincent.

Virgil:
From the Latin meaning "rod bearer, staff bearer."

Vladislav:
From the Polish *volod,* meaning "rule," and *slav,* meaning "glory."

U–V

W

Wade:
From the English meaning "ford."

Walden:
From the English meaning "wooded valley."

Walker:
From the English meaning "cloth worker."

Wallace:
From the Celtic meaning "Welshman" or the Old French meaning "foreign" or "stranger." *Alternative spelling:* Wallis.

Walter:
From the Old German meaning "ruling people." *Alternative spellings:* Walden, Waldo, Walther, Watkins. *Short forms:* Wal, Wally, Wat.

Ward:
From the English meaning "guardian" or "watchman."

Warren:
From the Old German meaning "guard."

Warwick:
From the English, meaning "buildings near the weir."

Wayland:
From the Old English meaning "land by the path."

Waylon:
From the English meaning "land beside the road."

Wayne:
From the Old English meaning "wagon maker" or the Old English meaning "meadow."

Wesley:
From the Old English meaning "west meadow."

Weston:
From the Old English meaning "west enclosure."

Wilbur:
From the Old English meaning "wall fortification" or "bright willow." *Alternative spelling:* Wilber. *Short forms:* Wil, Will, Willie, Willy.

Wilbert:
From the Old English meaning "well bright." *Short forms:* Wil, Will, Willie, Willy.

Wilfred:

From the Old English meaning "resolute" or the Old English meaning "wish for peace." *Alternative spelling:* Wilfrid. *Short forms:* Wil, Will, Willie, Willy.

Will:

See William.

Willard:

From the Old English meaning "hardy and resolute." *Short forms:* Wil, Will, Willie, Willy.

William:

From the Old German meaning "resolute protector." *Alternative spellings:* Guilaume, Guillaume, Liam, Quillermo, Vasilos, Vassos, Vilhelm, Welef, Wilhelm, Willem, Wilmer, Wilson. *Short forms:* Bill, Billy, Wil, Will, Willie, Willy.

Willie:

See William.

Wilmar:

From the Old German meaning "famous." *Alternative spelling:* Wilmer.

Wilson:

From the English, meaning "son of William."

Winfred:

From the Old English meaning "friend."

Winston:

From the Old English meaning "victorious town." *Short forms:* Win, Winnie.

Wolfgang:

From the Old German meaning "path of the wolf" or "traveling wolf." *Short forms:* Wolf, Wolfie.

Wyatt:

From the Old English meaning "water."

Wyn:

From the Welsh meaning "white," "pure," or "blessed." *Alternative spelling:* Wynne.

X–Y

Xander:
See Alexander.

Xavier:
From the Arabic meaning "splendid" or "bright" or the Basque meaning "owner of a new house." *Alternative spellings:* Javier, Zavier.

Xzavier:
The Basque form of Xavier.

Yael:
From the Hebrew meaning "mountain goat."

Yahir:
From the Spanish meaning "handsome."

Yair:
From the Hebrew meaning "he will enlighten."

Yandel:
A contemporary invented name.

Yosef:
See Joseph.

Yusuf:
The Arabic form of Joseph.

X–Y

90

Z

Zachariah:
From the Hebrew meaning "the Lord has remembered." *Alternative spelling:* Zechariah.

Zachary:
From the Hebrew meaning "God has remembered." *Alternative spellings:* Sachairi, Zacary, Zacharius, Zachery, Zackary, Zackery. *Short forms:* Zach, Zack.

Zaire:
From the Arabic name Sahir, meaning "shining, bright." Also the former name of the Democratic Republic of the Congo.

Zander:
See Alexander.

Zane:
See John. *Alternative spellings:* Zain, Zayne.

Zavier:
See Xavier.

Zayden:
Possibly a form of the Arabic name Zaid, meaning "increase" or "growth."

Zebedee:
From the Hebrew meaning "gift of God." *Alternative spelling:* Zebediah. *Short form:* Zeb.

Zedekiah:
From the Hebrew meaning "God is righteousness" or "God's justice." *Short form:* Zed.

Zeno:
From the Greek, meaning "gift of Zeus."

Zephaniah:
From the Hebrew origin, meaning "hidden by God."

Zeus:
From the Greek origin, meaning "living." The name of the chief of the Olympian gods.

Zion:
From the Hebrew meaning "highest point."

Zoltan:
From the Hungarian, meaning "life."

Girls' Names

A

Aaliyah:
See Aliya.

Abigail:
From the Hebrew meaning "father rejoices." *Alternative spellings:* Abagail, Abbigail, Abbrielle, Abigale, Abigayle. Avigail. *Short forms:* Abbie, Abby, Gail.

Abril:
From the French name Abrial, meaning "open, secure, protected."

Ada:
From the Old German meaning "noble." *Alternative spellings:* Addie, Aida, Eda.

Adah:
From the Hebrew meaning "beauty," "ornament."

Addison:
From the English meaning "son of Adam." *Alternative spelling:* Addisyn, Adison, Adyson.

Adelaide:
From the Old German meaning "noble sort." *Alternative spelling:* Adalind.

Adeline:
French form of Adelaide. *Alternative spelling:* Adaline, Adalyn, Adelyn.

Adriana:
The feminine form of Adrian (see Boys' Names). *Alternative spellings:* Adria, Adrianna, Adrianne.

Adrienne:
From the Latin and Greek meaning "rich," "black," or "mysterious." *Alternative spellings:* Adrien, Adrina.

Agatha:
From the Greek meaning "good," "kind." *Alternative spellings:* Agata, Aggie.

Aileen:
See Helen. *Alternative spellings:* Ailene, Aleen, Alena, Eileen, Eilidh, Elene. *Short forms:* Aila, Lena.

Aimee:
From the French meaning "beloved." *Alternative spelling:* Amy.

Ainsley:
From the English meaning "one's own meadow." *Alternative spellings:* Anslee, Ansley, Anslie.

Aisha:
From the Arabic meaning "prospering" or "woman." *Alternative spellings:* Aesha, Aiesha, Aishah, Aisia, Asha, Ahia, Ayeisha, Ayesha, Aysha, Ayshia.

A

Aiyana:
From the Native American meaning "forever flowering." *Alternative spelling:* Ayana.

Akira:
A contemporary invented name. A blend of A and Kira.

Alaina:
See Alana.

Alana:
From the Celtic meaning "distant place" or "fair," "beautiful." *Alternative spellings:* Alani, Alaina, Alanna, Alannah, Alayna. *Short form:* Lana.

Alanis:
The feminine form of Alan (see Boys' Names).

Aleah:
From the Arabic meaning "high, exulted."

Aleena:
A form of the Dutch name Aleene, meaning "alone." *Alternative spelling:* Alena.

Alessandra:
See Alexandra.

Alexandra:
The feminine form of Alexander (see Boys' Names). *Alternative spellings:* Alejandra, Alessandra. *Short forms:* Alex, Alexa. Olexa, Sacha, Sandra, Sandrine, Sasha, Xandra.

Alexia:
See Alexandra.

Alexis:
From the Greek meaning "helper." *Alternative spellings:* Alexus.

Aliana:
See Alana.

Alice:
From the Old German meaning "nobility." *Alternative spellings:* Alicia, Alison, Alissa, Alyssa, Alyssia, Allyce. *Short forms:* Ali, Allie, Ally.

Alicia:
See Alice.

Alina:
From the Arabic meaning "noble" or "illustrious."

Alisa:
From the Ancient Aramaic meaning "joy." *Alternative spelling:* Alissa, Alyssa, Aliza.

Alisha:
Possibly from the Arabic word *a'isha*, meaning "alive and well," or a form of Alicia. *Alternative spelling:* Allisha.

Alison:
See Alice. *Alternative spelling:* Allison, Allyson, Alyson.

Alivia:
See Olivia.

Aliya:
From the Hebrew meaning "ascender." *Alternative spellings:* Aaliyah, Aliyah.

Aliza:
From the Hebrew meaning "joyful."

Allie:
Familiar form of Alice, Alicia, Allison. *Alternative spelling:* Ally.

Alma:
From the Hebrew meaning "maiden" or the Latin meaning "kind."

Alondra:
A contemporary invented name. Possibly a form of Alexander.

Alyssa:
See Alisa. *Alternative spellings:* Allyssa.

Alyvia:
See Olivia.

Amanda:
From the Latin meaning "worthy of love," "loveable." *Short forms:* Manda, Mandee, Mandi, Mandie, Mandy.

Amani:
See Imani.

Amara:
From the Greek meaning "eternally beautiful." *Alternative spelling:* Amari.

Amaris:
From the Hebrew meaning "promised by God."

Amaya:
From the Japanese meaning "night rain."

Amber:
From the English word that denotes either the fossilized tree resin or the orange-yellow color. The word ultimately derives from the Arabic *anbar*.

Amelia:
From the Latin meaning "toil," "work." *Alternative spellings:* Amaline, Amalita, Emilia, Emily. *Short forms:* Ami, Amie, Amy, Em, Melia, Milly.

A

Amelie:
The french form of Amelia.

America:
A form of the Italian Amerigo, meaning "home ruler." The United States takes its nickname of "America" from Italian explorer Amerigo Vespucci.

Amina:
From the Arabic meaning "sure," "believable," "right," "trustworthy," "reliable," "dependable." *Alternative spelling:* Aminah.

Amira:
From the Hebrew meaning "speech" or the Arabic meaning "princess."

Amity:
From the Latin meaning "love" or "friendship."

Amiya:
See Amiyah.

Amiyah:
From the Sanskrit meaning "delight." *Alternative spelling:* Amiya

Amoura:
From the French meaning "love."

Amy:
From the French meaning "beloved"; see also Amelia, Ami, Amya. *Alternative spelling:* Ami.

Amya:
See Amy.

Ana:
The Spanish and Eastern European form of Hannah.

Anabelle:
See Annabelle. *Alternative spelling:* Anabel, Annabelle, Annabella.

Anahi:
From the Spanish meaning "beautiful like a flower."

Anaïs:
The Catalan Spanish version of Ana or Anne.

Anastasia:
From the Greek meaning "resurrection." *Short forms:* Nastasia, Stacey.

Anaya:
From the Sanskrit meaning "completely Free."

Andrea:

Possibly from the Greek meaning "womanly" or the feminine form of Andreas (see Boys' Names). *Alternative spellings:* Andra, Adreana, Andreea, Andria, Andrienne, Andrietta, Adrina, Androulla, Ondrea. *Short forms:* Andie, Andre, Andrie, Andy, Dreena, Drena, Drina, Rena, Rina.

Angel:

From the Greek meaning "angel" or the Latin meaning "messenger."

Angela:

From the Greek meaning "messenger." *Alternative spellings:* Angelia, Angeline. *Short forms:* Angel, Angie.

Angelica:

From the Latin *angelicus*, meaning "angelic" or the French meaning "like an angel." *Short forms:* Angel, Angie.

Angelina:

See Angela. *Alternative spelling:* Angeline.

Angelique:

The French form of Angelica.

Anika:

From the African meaning "smart," "beautiful," or "child of god."

Anita:

See Anne. *Short form:* Nita.

Aniya:

See Anne. *Alternative spelling:* Aniyah.

Aniyah:

See Aniya.

Ann:

See Anne.

Anna:

See Anne.

Annabelle:

A blend of Anna and Belle. *Alternative spelling:* Anabel, Anabelle, Annabella.

Annalise:

A contemporary invented name. A blend of Anna and Lise.

A

Anne:
From the Hebrew meaning "grace" or "favored." *Alternative spellings: Ana, Anaïs, Anci, Andula, Andulka, Anette, Anicka, Ania, Anita, Aniya, Aniyah, Ann, Anna, Annchen, Anneli, Anneke, Annette, Anni, Annie, Anny, Anouk, Anya, Hanna, Hannah, Hanne, Nan, Nana, Nani, Nancy, Nanna, Nina, Ninon, Nita, Noula.*

Anneliese:
From the Latin meaning "graced with God's bounty." *Alternative spelling:* Annaliese.

Annette:
See Anne. *Short form:* Anne, Annie, Netta, Nettie.

Annika:
The Russian form of Ann.

Ansley:
See Ainsley.

Anthea:
From the Greek *antheios,* meaning "flowery."

Antoinette:
See Antonia.

Antonia:
The feminine form of Anthony (see Boys' Names). *Alternative spellings:* Antoineta, Antoinsetta, Antoinette, Antonie. *Short forms:* Anna, Ant, Nina, Netta, Netti, Toinetta, Toinette, Toni, Tonia, Toney, Tony.

Anya:
See Anne.

April:
From the Latin meaning "opening." *Alternative spelling:* Avril.

Arabella:
From the Latin meaning "beautiful altar" or the German meaning "eagle." *Short forms:* Bel, Bella.

Araceli:
From the Spanish meaning "heavenly altar." *Alternative spelling:* Aracely.

Areli:
See Oralee. *Alternative spelling:* Arely.

Aria:
From the Italian meaning "a melody."

Arianna:
From the Welsh *arian,* meaning "silver." *Alternative spelling:* Ariana.

Arianne:
From the Greek meaning "the very holy" or "pleasing one." *Alternative spelling:* Ariane.

Ariel:
From the Hebrew meaning "lion of God." *Alternative spellings:* Arielle, Ariela. *Short form:* Ari.

Armani:
From the Persian meaning "desire, goal." Also an Italian surname.

Aryana:
See Arianna. *Alternative spelling:* Aryanna.

Asa:
From the Japanese meaning "born in the morning" or the Hebrew meaning "doctor," "healer."

Ashanti:
From the name of an African tribe.

Ashley:
From the Old English meaning "ash tree meadow." *Alternative spellings:* Ashlee, Ashleigh, Ashli, Ashlie, Ashly, Ashlyn, Ashlynn.

Ashlyn:
From the English meaning "ash tree pool." *Alternative spelling:* Ashlynn.

Asia:
From the Greek meaning "resurrection." Also the Continent of that name.

Aspen:
From the English meaning "aspen tree." A City in Colorado.

Astra:
From the Greek meaning "star."

Astrid:
From the Scandinavian *áss*, meaning "god," and *frior*, meaning "fair," or possibly the Old Norse meaning "divine strength."

Athena:
From the Greek meaning "wise."

Aubree:
See Aubrey.

Aubrey:
From the German meaning "noble"; the French meaning "blonde ruler"; or possibly from *alb*, meaning "elf," and *ric*, meaning "power." *Alternative spelling:* Aubree, Aubrie.

A

Audrey:
From the Old English name *Ethelreda,* meaning "strength." *Alternative spellings:* Audey, Audi, Audree, Audri, Audrie, Audry.

Audrina:
See Audrey.

Augusta:
From the Latin meaning "venerable."

Aurelia:
From the Latin meaning "golden." *Alternative spelling:* Oralia.

Aurora:
From the Latin meaning "dawn."

Autumn:
From the English meaning "season of harvest." It is the fall season.

Ava:
From the Latin meaning "bird."

Avery:
From the old English meaning "ruler of the elves." *Alternative spelling:* Averie.

Avis:
From the Old German meaning "refuge in war" or the Latin meaning "bird." *Short form:* Ava.

Avril:
See April.

Ayana:
See Aiyana.

Ayanna:
From the Hindi meaning "innocent."

Ayesha:
See Aisha.

Ayla:
From the Hebrew meaning "oak tree."

Aylin:
See Alina.

Azaria:
From the Hebrew meaning "aided by God."

Azul:
From the Arabic meaning "color of the sky without clouds."

B

Bailey:
See Boys' Names. *Alternative spellings:* Bailee, Baylee, Bayleigh.

Bambi:
From the Italian meaning "little child."

Barbara:
From the Latin meaning "foreign" or "stranger." *Alternative spelling:* Barbera. *Short forms:* Babs, Barb.

Bathsheba:
From the Hebrew meaning "daughter of opulence" or "daughter of an oath." *Alternative spelling:* Batsheba. *Short form:* Sheba.

Batya:
From the Hebrew meaning "daughter of God."

Beatrice:
The Italian and French form of Beatrix.

Beatrix:
From the Latin meaning "bringer of happiness." *Alternative spellings:* Beatriks, Beatrise, Beitris, Betrys. *Short forms:* Bea, Bee, Trixie, Trixy.

Becky:
See Rebecca.

Belen:
From the Spanish meaning "at Bethlehem."

Belinda:
From the Old English meaning "very beautiful" or the Old Spanish meaning "pretty."

Bella:
From the Latin meaning "fair," "lovely one"; see also Arabella or Isabelle. *Alternative spelling:* Belle.

Benita:
From the Latin meaning "blessed."

Bernadette:
From the German, meaning "bold as a bear." The feminine form of Bernard (see Boys' Names). *Alternative spelling:* Bernadete. *Short form:* Bernie

B

Bernice:
From the Greek meaning "bringer of victory." *Alternative spelling:* Berenice.

Bertha:
From the Old German meaning "bright." *Alternative spelling:* Bertina.

Beryl:
From the Greek meaning "sea green jewel"; the Sanskrit meaning "precious stone," or the Arabic meaning "crystal" or "very clear."

Bess:
See Elizabeth.

Beth:
From the Hebrew meaning "house"; see also Elizabeth.

Bethag:
From the Gaelic meaning "life."

Bethan:
See Elizabeth.

Bethany:
Possibly from the Hebrew *beth te'ena,* meaning "house of figs," or the Aramaic meaning "house of poverty."

Betsy:
See Elizabeth.

Betty:
See Elizabeth.

Beulah:
From the Hebrew meaning "claimed as wife" or "she who is to be married/ruled over."

Beverly:
From the Old English meaning "beaver meadow."

Bevin:
From the Irish Gaelic meaning "sweet-singing maiden." *Alternative spelling:* Béibhinn.

Beyonce:
Of contemporary origin. An invented name.

Bianca:
From the Italian meaning "white" or "pure." *Alternative spelling:* Blanche.

Bibi:
From the French meaning "toy" or "bauble" or the Arabic meaning "lady."

Bijou:
From the French meaning "jewel."

Billie:
See Wilhelmina.

Bina:
From the Hebrew meaning "wise" and "understanding."

Binnie:
From the Celtic meaning "crib," "wicker basket."

Blair:
From the Scottish Gaelic meaning "from the flat/level place."

Blake:
From the English meaning "black."

Blanca:
From the Spanish meaning "white."

Blanche:
From the French meaning "white."
Alternative spellings: Bianca, Blanca, Branka.

Bliss:
From the Old English meaning "happiness," "joy."

Blodwedd:
From the Welsh meaning "flower face."

Blodwen:
From the Welsh meaning "white flower."

Blossom:
From the Old English meaning "a plant or tree in flower."

Blythe:
From the English blithe, meaning "happy," or "cheerful."

Bo:
From the Chinese meaning "precious" or the Old Norse meaning "householder."

Bobbie:
See Roberta.

Bonita:
From the Spanish meaning "little good one" or "pretty."

Bonnie:
From the Latin meaning "good."

Braelyn:
A contemporary invented name. A blend of Braeden (see boys names) and Lynn.

B

Brandy:

Possibly a feminine form of the name Brandon (see Boys' Names); from the Old English meaning "to burn wine"; from the fortified wine, or from the Italian surname Brand meaning "sword." *Alternative spelling:* Brandi.

Breda:

See Bridget.

Bree:

From the Middle English meaning "broth" or the Irish meaning "hill."

Breeya:

From the Gaelic *brigh* meaning "strength" or "force."

Brenda:

The feminine form of Brendan (see Boys' Names) or from the Scandinavian *brand,* meaning "burning sword," or the Irish meaning "princess." *Alternative spelling:* Brenna.

Brenna:

See Brenda.

Bria:

See Briana.

Brianna:

Feminine form of Brian (see Boys' Names). *Alternative spellings:* Breana, Breanna, Bria, Briana, Brianne, Brina, Bryana, Bryanna, Bryanne.

Brice:

See Boys' Names. *Alternative spelling:* Bryce.

Bridget:

From the Celtic meaning "strength" or "high." *Alternative spelling:* Breda.

Brielle:

A contemporary invented name. A short form of Gabrielle.

Brigette:

From the Irish meaning "bold" or "strong." *Alternative spellings:* Brigit, Bridgeda.

Briley:

A contemporary invented name. A blend of Brianna and Riley. *Alternative spelling:* Brylee.

Briony:

From the Greek *bryonia,* meaning "climbing vine." *Alternative spelling:* Bryony. *Short form:* Bry.

Brisa:
From the Spanish meaning "beloved."

Britt:
From the Scandinavian meaning "strength."

Britta:
From the Old English meaning "pride."

Brittany:
From the Latin meaning "from Britain." *Alternative spellings:* Britney, Brittney.

Brooke:
From the Old English *broc,* meaning "water," "stream."

Brooklyn:
From the area of New York City. *Alternative spelling:* Brooklynn.

Brunhild:
From the Old High German meaning "someone well-prepared for life's struggle" or "armored warrior."

Bryanna:
See Brianna.

Bryce:
See Brice.

Brylee:
See Briley.

Brynn:
From the Welsh meaning "hill" or "mountain." *Alternative spelling:* Bryn.

Bryna:
From the Irish Gaelic meaning "strength."

Bryony:
From the Greek, meaning "climbing plant." *Alternative spelling:* Brioni, Briony, Bryonie.

Buffy:
From the American buffalo meaning "from the plains" or a pet form of Elizabeth.

C

Cadence:
From the Latin meaning "rhythm, beat." *Alternative spelling:* Kaydence.

Cailyn:
A form of Caitlin.

Caitlin:
The Gaelic form of Catherine. *Alternative spellings:* Caitlyn, Katelyn, Kathleen.

Calista:
From the Greek meaning "most beautiful." *Alternative spelling:* Callista.

Callan:
From the Gaelic, meaning "powerful in battle." *Alternative spellings:* Kallan.

Callie:
See Caroline. *Alternative spelling:* Cali.

Calpurnia:
Name of Caesar's wife in Shakespearian play.

Calypso:
From the Greek meaning "concealer" or "to conceal."

Camelia:
See Camilla.

Cameo:
From the Italian meaning "jewel."

Cameron:
From the Scottish meaning "crooked nose." *Alternative spellings:* Camryn, Kameron, Kamryn. *Short forms:* Cam.

Camilla:
From the Latin meaning "attendant at a sacrifice/ceremony." *Alternative spellings:* Camelia, Camille, Kamilla. *Short forms:* Cam, Cami, Cammi, Cammie, Cammy, Milli, Millie, Milly.

Camille:
See Camilla.

Campbell:
From the Latin meaning "beautiful field" or the Scottish meaning "crooked mouth."

Camryn:
See Cameron.

Candace:
From the Greek meaning "glittering white," "glowing." *Alternative spellings:* Candice, Candida. *Short form:* Candy.

Candice:
See Candace.

Candida:
See Candace.

Candy:
See Candace.

Caprice:
From the French meaning "whimsical" or "unpredictable" or the Italian meaning "fanciful."

Cara:
From the Gaelic meaning "friend" or the Latin meaning "dear." *Alternative spellings:* Careen, Carey.

Careen:
See Cara.

Caresse:
From the French meaning "tender touch."

Carey:
See Cara or Caroline. *Alternative spelling:* Carrie.

Caridad:
From the Spanish meaning "charity."

Carina:
From the Italian meaning "dear little one." *Alternative spelling:* Karina.

Carissa:
From the Latin meaning "dear one." *Alternative spellings:* Caressa, Carice, Carisa, Karessa, Karisa, Karissa. *Short forms:* Cari, Carie.

Carita:
From the Latin meaning "kindness."

Carla:
From the Old German meaning "free woman." *Alternative spellings:* Carleia, Carlene, Carley, Carlie, Carly, Karla.

Carlene:
See Carla.

Carlin:
See Caroline.

Carlotta:
See Charlotte. *Short form:* Lola.

C

Carly:
See Carla. *Alternative spellings:* Carlee, Carley, Carlie, Karlie, Karly.

Carmel:
From the Hebrew meaning "the garden."

Carmela:
From the Latin meaning "fruitful orchard." *Alternative spelling:* Carmella.

Carmen:
From the Latin meaning "song." *Alternative spelling:* Charmaine.

Carol:
From the Old French meaning "to celebrate in song" or possibly the Latin meaning "strong and womanly"; see also Caroline.

Carolina:
See Caroline.

Caroline:
A feminine form of Charles (see Boys' Names). *Alternative spellings:* Carlin, Carolina, Carolyn, Carolyne, Karoline. *Short forms:* Carol, Carrie.

Carrie:
See Caroline. *Alternative spelling:* Karrie.

Caryon:
See Catherine.

Carys:
From the Welsh meaning "love" or possibly "helper of men." *Alternative spellings:* Caris, Ceri, Cerise, Cerys.

Casey:
From the Irish meaning "brave in battle." *Alternative spelling:* Kasey.

Cassandra:
From the Greek meaning "the confuser of men." *Alternative spelling:* Kassandra. *Short forms:* Cass, Cassie, Cassy, Sandi, Sandra.

Cassia:
From the Greek meaning "herb."

Cassidy:
From the Irish meaning "curly headed" or "clever." *Alternative spellings:* Kassady, Kassidy. *Short forms:* Cass, Cassie.

Cassie:
See Cassandra.

Catalina:
The Spanish form of Catherine.

Cate:
See Catherine.

Catherine:
From the Greek *katharos,* meaning "pure." *Alternative spellings:* Caitlin, Caryon, Catalina, Cathleen, Cathryn, Catriona, Kaitlin, Katalina, Katarina, Katena, Katerina, Katharin, Katharine, Katherine, Kathleen, Kathrin, Kathrine, Kathryn, Kathryne, Kathrynn, Katrla, Katriana, Katriane, Katrina, Katrine, Katina, Katrya. *Short forms:* Cate, Catrina, Kara, Karen, Karesa, Karina, Kate, Katie, Kitty, Kathy, Kathie.

Cathleen:
See Catherine.

Catrina:
See Catherine.

Catriona:
See Catherine.

Cayla:
See Kay.

Cecilia:
The feminine form of Cecil (see Boys' Names). *Alternative spellings:* Cecelia, Cecile, Cicely, Cissy, Sisley.

Cedra:
Possibly the feminine version of Cedric (see Boys' Names).

Celeste:
From the Latin meaning "heavenly." *Alternative spellings:* Celesta, Celestin, Celestina, Celestine. *Short forms:* Cela, Cella, Celle, Cesla, Tyna.

Celia:
From the Latin *caelum,* meaning "heaven"; see also Celeste.

Celine:
From the Latin meaning "heaven" or the Greek meaning "moon." *Alternative spellings:* Celene, Celina, Salena, Selene, Selina, Sheila.

Ceres:
From the Latin meaning "of the spring."

Ceri:
See Carys.

Cerise:
From the French meaning "cherry."

Cerys:
See Carys.

C

Chandra:
From the Hindu god of the moon or the Sanskrit meaning "moon."

Chanel:
Possibly from the Old French *chandele,* meaning "candle maker"; also after Coco Chanel.

Chantal:
From the French meaning "singer." *Alternative spelling:* Chantelle.

Charis:
From the Greek meaning "grace," "kindness."

Charity:
From the Latin meaning "benevolent goodwill and hope" or the Latin *caritas,* meaning "caring for and loving others."

Charlee:
See Charlotte.

Charlene:
A feminine form of Charles (see Boys' Names). *Alternative spelling:* Sharlene.

Charlie:
See Charlotte.

Charlize:
See Charlotte.

Charlotte:
From the Old German meaning "free woman" or "small woman." *Alternative spellings:* Carla, Carlotta, Charlene, Charlet, Charletta, Charlette, Charline, Charlott, Charlotta, Charlotty, Charmaine, Charolet, Charolette. *Short forms:* Carly, Char, Chara, Charl, Charla, Charle, Charlie, Charlisa, Charlita, Charlo, Lots, Lotte, Lottie, Lotty.

Charmaine:
From the Roman clan name Carmineus; the Greek meaning "mother of joy"; or possibly the Latin meaning "a singer"; see also Carmen. *Alternative spelling:* Charmain.

Chastity:
From the Latin meaning "purity," "innocence."

Chaya:
From the Hebrew meaning "life."

Chelsea:
From the Old English meaning "ship's port" or possibly from the area of London. *Alternative spelling:* Chelsey.

Cher:
From the French meaning "beloved."

Cherie:
From the French *chérie,* meaning "dear or love." *Alternative spellings:* Charlene, Cheri, Cheryl.

Cherish:
From the English meaning "dearly beloved."

Cherry:
From the fruit.

Cheryl:
Possibly from the French *chérie,* meaning "dear." *Alternative spelling:* Sheryl.

Chesna:
From the Slavic meaning "peaceful."

Chessa:
From the Slavic meaning "at peace."

Cheyenne:
From the name of a Native American tribe. *Alternative spelling:* Shyann, Shyanne.

Chiara:
The Italian form of Clare. *Alternative spelling:* Kira.

Chloe:
From the Greek meaning "a green shoot," "fresh blooming," "verdant." *Alternative spelling:* Cloe, Khloe.

Chloris:
From the Greek meaning "pale."

Chris:
See Christina.

Christa:
See Christina.

Christabel:
From the Latin and French, meaning is "beautiful Christian." *Alternative spellings:* Christabell, Chrystabel, Chrystabelle, Cristabel, Cristabell, Crystabel.

Christie:
See Christina.

Christina:
From the Greek or Latin meaning "Christian." *Alternative spellings:* Christabel, Christel, Christen, Christine, Kirsten, Kirstin, Kristen, Kristina. *Short forms:* Chris, Chrissy, Christa, Christie, Crista, Christy, Ina, Kirsty, Kris, Krista, Kristi, Kristie, Kristy, Tina.

C

Christine:
See Christina.

Christy:
See Christina.

Chrysanthe:
From the Greek meaning "precious flower." *Alternative spelling:* Chrysantha.

Ciara:
From the Irish meaning "black-haired." *Alternative spelling:* Cierra. The Irish feminine form of Ciaran (see Boys' Names). *Alternative spellings:* Ciar, Kara, Keira, Kiara, Kiera.

Cicely:
See Cecelia.

Cilla:
See Priscilla.

Cindy:
See Cynthia or Lucinda.

Cira:
A feminine form of Cyril (see Boys' Names). *Alternative spelling:* Kira.

Cissy:
See Cecilia.

Claire:
From the Latin meaning "famous." *Alternative spellings:* Chiara, Clair, Clairine, Clare, Clarine, Clarita, Clarissa.

Clara:
From the Latin meaning "clear," "bright."

Claribel:
From the English meaning "bright," "beautiful." *Alternative spelling:* Clarabelle.

Clarice:
See Clarissa. *Alternative spelling:* Clarise.

Clarissa:
From the Greek meaning "brilliant"; see also Clare. *Alternative spelling:* Klarissa. *Short forms:* Clarice, Clarise.

Claudette:
See Claudia.

Claudia:
From the Latin meaning "lame." *Alternative spellings:* Claudette, Claudine. *Short forms:* Claudi, Claudie.

114

Clea:
See Cleo.

Clemency:
From the Latin meaning "mildness."

Clementine:
From the Latin meaning "merciful."

Cleo:
From the Greek meaning "glory"; see also Cleopatra. *Alternative spelling:* Clea.

Cleopatra:
From the Greek meaning "glory of her father." *Short form:* Cleo.

Clio:
From the Greek meaning "proclaimer," "glorifier."

Clodagh:
From the Irish. Of recent coinage, and based on a place and river name.

Cloe:
See Chloe.

Clotilda:
From the German meaning "heroine" or the Old German meaning "loud battle."

Cody:
From the Irish meaning "helpful."
Alternative spellings: Codey, Codi, Codie, Kodey, Kodi, Kodie, Kody.

Coleen:
From the Irish meaning "girl." *Alternative spellings:* Colleen, Cailin.

Colette:
The feminine form of Colin (see Boys' Names); see also Nicole. *Alternative spelling:* Collette.

Colleen:
From the Irish meaning "girl." *Alternative spellings:* Colene, Coline, Collen, Collene, Colline.

Connie:
See Constance.

Constance:
From the Latin meaning "faithful." *Alternative spellings:* Constancia, Constanta, Constantia, Constanz, Konstance, Konstantin, Konstanze. *Short forms:* Con, Conni, Connie, Conny.

Consuelo:
From the Latin meaning "consolation."

C

Cora:
Possibly from the Greek *kore,* meaning "maiden." *Alternative spellings:* Coretta, Corey, Cory, Kora.

Coral:
From the Latin meaning "from the sea."

Cordelia:
From the Latin meaning "warm-hearted," "good-hearted"; the Welsh meaning "sea jewel"; or the Celtic meaning "daughter of the sea."

Corentine:
See Corinna.

Coretta:
See Cora.

Corinne:
From the Greek *korinna,* meaning "maiden." *Alternative spellings:* Corentine, Corina, Corinne. *Short forms:* Corey, Cory, Cri, Kore.

Cornelia:
Feminine form of Cornelius (see Boys' Names).

Cory:
See Cora. *Alternative spelling:* Corey.

Courtney:
Possibly from the Old English meaning "court dweller" or "from the court" or the English meaning "courteous."

Cressida:
From the Greek meaning "golden one."

Cristina:
See Christina.

Crystal:
From the French meaning "clear" or "brilliant." *Alternative spellings:* Cristal, Cristel, Krystal.

Cybil:
From the Greek meaning "prophet." *Alternative spellings:* Cybele, Sibyl, Sybyl.

Cynthia:
From Kynthia, the Greek goddess of wild animals or from the Greek meaning "moon"; see also Sancha. *Alternative spellings:* Cynthiana, Cynthie, Hyacinth, Kynthia. *Short forms:* Cinda, Cindee, Cindi, Cindie, Cindy, Cyndie, Cyndy, Cynth, Kynthia, Sindee, Sindy, Tia.

D

Dahlia:
From the Scandinavian meaning "valley" or the flower.

Daisy:
From the Old English meaning "day's eye" or the flower. *Alternative spellings:* Daisia, Daisie, Dasey, Dasi, Dasie, Daysee, Daysie, Daysy.

Dakota:
From the Native American Sioux meaning "friend."

Dalia:
From the Arabic meaning "gentle."

Damaris:
From the Greek meaning "heifer" or "calf," implying gentleness, or the Latin meaning "gentle."

Dana:
From the Celtic "Queen of the Danes" or "from Denmark." *Alternative spellings:* Daina, Dane, Danna, Dansy, Dayna.

Dania:
See Daniela.

Danica:
From the Norse meaning "morning star." *Alternative spelling:* Danika.

Daniela:
From the Hebrew meaning "God has judged." *Alternative spellings:* Dania, Daniella, Danielle. *Short form:* Dana.

Danielle:
See Daniela. *Alternative spelling:* Daniele.

Danita:
Possibly from the Latin meaning "given by God." *Alternative spellings:* Danicka, Danuta.

Danna:
See Dana.

Daphne:
From the Greek meaning "laurel bush" or "bay tree." *Alternative spellings:* Daphna, Daphnee.

D

Davina:
From the Hebrew meaning "beloved."

Dawn:
From the English meaning "daybreak."

Dayana:
See Dianna.

Dayanara:
From the Greek meaning "she stirs up great passions." *Alternative spelling:* Dayanira.

Deanna:
From the Latin meaning "bright as day" or the Old English meaning "from the valley."

Deborah:
From the Hebrew meaning "wisdom." *Alternative spellings:* Debora, Decora, Devera, Devorah, Devrah. *Short forms:* Deb, Debbi, Debbie, Debo, Debra, Dedra, Deidra, Deidre.

Decima:
The feminine form of Decimus (see Boys' Names).

Dee:
From the Welsh meaning "black," "dark."

Deirdre:
From the Celtic meaning "one who rages"; the Gaelic meaning "broken-hearted" or the Middle English meaning "young girl." *Alternative spellings:* Deidra, Dedra, Deidrie, Diedre.

Deja:
From the French meaning "already."

Dela:
See Adela.

Delaney:
From the Irish meaning "defender of the challenger."

Delia:
From the Greek meaning "born on the island of Delos."

Delicia:
From the Latin meaning "to give pleasure" or "to charm."

Delilah:
From the Arabic meaning "guide" or "leader" or the Hebrew meaning "poor" or "hair."

Demi:
From the French meaning "half."

Dena:
From the Anglo-Saxon meaning "glen."
Alternative spelling: Denna.

Denise:
The feminine form of Denis (see Boys' Names).

Dervla:
From the Irish meaning "daughter of the poet."

Desdemona:
From the Greek meaning "woman of bad fortune."

Desirae:
See Desiree.

Desirée:
From the Old French meaning "hope" or "desired." *Alternative spelling:* Desirae.

Desma:
From the Greek meaning "bond," "pledge."

Desta:
From the French "destiny."

Destiny:
From the French meaning "fate."
Alternative spellings: Destinee, Destini.

Deva:
From the Sanskrit meaning "god," "divine."

Devi:
From the Hindi meaning "goddess."

Devon:
See Boys' Names.

Devyn:
See Devon.

Dextra:
From the Latin meaning "right-hand side."

Diamanta:
From the Greek meaning "unconquerable."

Diamond:
From the English meaning "precious, brilliant gem."

Diana:
From the Latin *dius,* meaning "god like," "divine." *Alternative spellings:* Deana, Deanna, Dianna, Dianne, Dyann. *Short forms:* Dee, Di, Dian.

Dilys:
From the Welsh meaning "genuine," "perfect," "true."

D

Dinah:
From the Hebrew meaning "vindication" or "judgement."

Dione:
From the Greek meaning "divine queen." *Alternative spellings:* Dion, Dionis, Dionne.

Dionisia:
A feminine form of Dionysus (see Boys' Names).

Dionne:
See Dione.

Dita:
See Edith.

Diva:
From the Latin meaning "goddess."

Divina:
From the Latin meaning "divine one."

Dixie:
From the Old Norse meaning "active spirit."

Diya:
From the Hindi meaning "dazzling personality."

Dolores:
From the Spanish meaning "grief," "lady of sorrows." *Alternative spellings:* Lolita. *Short forms:* Dela, Dol, Lola.

Dominica:
From the Latin meaning "born on the Sabbath." *Short forms:* Dom, Doma, Domin, Dominiee, Nica, Nika.

Dominique:
From the Latin meaning "belonging to God." *Alternative spellings:* Dominica, Dominick, Dominik, Dominika. *Short forms:* Dom, Doma, Domin, Dominiee, Nica, Nika.

Donalda:
The feminine form of Donald (see Boys' Names). *Alternative spellings:* Donella, Donelle, Donnelle.

Donata:
From the Latin meaning "gift" or "deserving of gifts."

Donella:
See Donalda. *Alternative spelling:* Donnelle.

Donna:
From the Italian meaning "lady."

Dora:
See Dorothea.

Doreen:
See Dorothea.

Dorian:
Possibly from the Greek meaning "child of the sea."

Doris:
From the Greek meaning "bountiful," "from the ocean," or "sacrificial knife."

Dorit:
From the Hebrew *dor*, meaning "generation." *Alternative spellings:* Doritt, Dorrit.

Dorothea:
From the Greek meaning "gift of God," "divine gift." *Alternative spellings:* Doraleen, Doreen, Dorene, Dorita, Dorothy, Dorrie, Dortha, Dorthy, Dory, Drinda. *Short forms:* Dodi, Dodo, Dollie, Dolly, Dora, Dorat, Dori, Dory, Dot, Dotti, Dottie, Dotty, Thea.

Drew:
A feminine form of Andrew (see Boys' Names).

Druella:
From the Old German meaning "elfin vision."

Drusilla:
From the Greek meaning "soft-eyed" or the Latin meaning "firm" or "the strong one." *Alternative spelling:* Drucie. *Short forms:* Dru, Druci.

Dryden:
From the Old English meaning "dry valley" or "dry land."

Dulce:
From the Latin meaning "sweet."

Dulcie:
From the Latin meaning "sweet."

Dusty:
The feminine form of Dustin (see Boys' Names).

Dylan:
From the Welsh meaning "son of the sea."

E

Ea:
From the Greek, possibly the name of or meaning "a goddess."

Eartha:
Possibly from the Old English meaning "child of the earth."

Ebony:
From the Latin or Greek meaning "dark," "black." *Alternative spellings:* Eboni, Ebonie.

Eden:
From the Hebrew meaning "delightful, earthly paradise."

Edith:
From the Old English *ead,* meaning "wealthy" or "fortunate," and *gyo,* meaning "war." *Alternative spellings:* Edine, Editha, Edithe, Eidita. *Short forms:* Eade, Eda, Edda, Edie, Edy, Dita.

Edna:
From the Hebrew meaning "pleasure"; see also Ada.

Eileen:
See Helen. *Alternative spellings:* Aileen, Eilean, Eileen, Eilene, Ilene.

Eileigh:
Gaelic form of Helen.

Eilidh:
The Gaelic form of Aileen.

Eira:
From the Welsh meaning "snow."

Eireen:
See Irene.

Elaina:
See Elaine.

Elaine:
From the Italian name Elettre, which comes from the Greek *elektor,* meaning "brilliant"; see also Helen. *Alternative spellings:* Elana, Elayne.

Eleanor:

See Helen. *Alternative spellings:* Elana, Elanor, Eleanour, Eleanora, Eleanore, Elena, Elenore, Elinor, Elinore, Ellinore, Elnore, Elynor, Elynore, Nell, Noreen, Leonora, Leonore, Lunore. *Short forms:* Ellie, Nel, Nora.

Elen:

From the Welsh meaning "nymph"; see also Helen. *Alternative spellings:* Elin, Elan, Ellen, Nel.

Elena:

The Spanish form of Helen.

Elfrida:

Possibly the feminine form of Alfred (see Boys' Names). *Short forms:* Freda, Frida.

Eliana:

From the Hebrew meaning "my God has answered me." *Alternative spelling:* Elliana.

Elin:

See Elen.

Elisa:

See Elizabeth. *Alternative spelling:* Eliza.

Elise:

See Elizabeth. *Alternative spelling:* Elyse.

Elizabeth:

From the Hebrew meaning "oath of God." *Alternative spellings:* Elisabet, Elisabeth, Elisveta. *Short forms:* Bess, Bessi, Bessie, Bessy, Bet, Beta, Beth, Bethan, Betka, Betsi, Betsy, Bett, Betta, Bette, Bettina, Betty, Betuska, Buffy, Ela, Elsa, Elsbeth, Elisa, Elise, Elissa, Eliza, Ellie, Elsa, Else, Elsi, Elsie, Elspeth, Eylse, Eylssa, Ilse, Isa, Isabella, Isabelle, Libbi, Libbie, Libby, Liese, Liesel, Lisa, Lisbet, Lisbeth, Lise, Lisette, Liz, Liza, Lizabeth, Lizbeth, Lizette, Lizzi, Lizzie, Lizzy.

Ella:

From the Old German meaning "all" or the English meaning "elfin" or "beautiful fairy woman." *Short form:* Ellie.

Elle:

From the French meaning "she." Also a short form of Eleanor, Ella.

Ellen:

See Elen or Helen. *Short form:* Nell.

Ellie:

Short form of Ella, Elizabeth, Eleanor, or Elen. *Alternative spelling:* Elly.

E

Elsa:
See Elizabeth.

Elsie:
See Elizabeth.

Elspeth:
See Elizabeth.

Eluned:
From the Welsh meaning "icon."

Elvira:
From the German *ali,* meaning "other," and *wer,* meaning "true"; the Latin meaning "white" or "blonde"; the Spanish meaning "elfin"; the German meaning "closed up"; or the Old German *alverat,* meaning "wise counsel."

Elyse:
See Elise.

Emerson:
From the German meaning "son of the chief."

Emery:
From the German meaning "industrious."

Emilia:
See Amelia, Emily.

Emily:
From the Latin meaning "flatterer"; the German meaning "industrious"; or the Roman clan name Aemilius. *Alternative spellings:* Em, Ema, Emaily, Emeli, Emeline, Emely, Emilee, Emili, Emilia, Emilienne, Emmalee, Emmalou, Emma, Emmie. See also Amelia.

Emma:
From the German meaning "universal," "whole," or "complete"; see also Emily.

Emmy:
See Emily.

Erica:
The feminine version of Eric (see Boys' Names). *Alternative spelling:* Erika.

Erin:
From the Irish meaning "Ireland" or the Old Norse meaning "peace."

Ermintrude:
From the Old German *ermin,* meaning "whole" or "universe," and *drudi,* meaning "strength."

Erna:
From the German form of Ernesta.

Ernesta:
The feminine form of Ernest (see Boys' Names). *Alternative spelling:* Ernestine. *Short form:* Erna.

Esmé:
From the French meaning "esteemed"; see also Esmeralda.

Esmeralda:
From the Spanish meaning "emerald." *Alternative spelling:* Esmerelda. *Short form:* Esmé.

Esperanza:
From the Spanish meaning "hope, expectation."

Essence:
From the Latin meaning "life, existence."

Estelle:
From the French meaning "star." *Alternative spelling:* Estella. *Short forms:* Stella, Stelle.

Esther:
From the Hebrew *hadassah,* meaning "myrtle," or the Persian *esthar,* meaning "evening star." *Alternative spellings:* Ester, Hester, Hetty. *Short forms:* Essa, Essi, Essy, Esta, Etti, Ettie, Etty.

Estrella:
From the Spanish meaning "star."

Eva:
See Eve.

Evangeline:
From the Greek meaning "one who proclaims the gospel" or "good news." *Alternative spelling:* Evangelina. *Short forms:* Eve, Eva.

Eve:
From the Hebrew *chavah,* meaning "life giving" or "life." *Alternative spellings:* Aoiffe, Chava, Eba, Ebba, Eva, Evelin, Evolina, Evolyn, Evi, Evia, Evioka, Evin, Evita, Evka, Evlun, Ewa, Ina, Lina.

Evelyn:
From the English, Old German, or French meaning "hazelnut"; see also Eve. *Alternative spellings:* Aveline, Evaline, Evelin, Evelynne, Evline, Evlyne.

Evette:
See Yvonne.

Evie:
See Eve.

F

Faith:
From the Latin meaning "trust" or "devotion."

Fallon:
From the Irish surname meaning "leader" or "grandchild of the ruler."

Farah:
From the Arabic meaning "joy" or "cheerfulness."

Farrah:
From the Middle English meaning "beautiful" or "pleasant" or the Arabic meaning "happiness."

Fatima:
From the Arabic meaning "gentle" or "chaste."

Fawn:
From the French meaning "young deer."

Fay:
From the French meaning "fairy." *Alternative spellings:* Fae, Faye.

Felicia:
From the Latin meaning "lucky." *Alternative spelling:* Phylicia.

Felicity:
From the Latin meaning "happiness."

Fenella:
From the Gaelic meaning "white shoulder." *Alternative spellings:* Finella, Finola, Finnoula, Fionnuala, Fionnula. *Short forms:* Nola, Nuala.

Fern:
From the plant.

Fernanda:
From the German meaning "daring, adventurous."

Ffion:
From the Welsh meaning "foxglove flower."

Finley:
From the Irish meaning "fair-haired hero." Also see Finlay in Boys' Names.

Finola:
See Fenella.

Fiona:
From the Gaelic meaning "fair" or "white." *Short form:* Fi.

Fleur:
From the French meaning "flower."

Flor:
From the Spanish meaning "flower."

Flora:
From the Latin meaning "flower." *Short forms:* Flo, Florry.

Florence:
From the Latin meaning "blooming" or "flourishing." *Short forms:* Flo, Florry.

Fran:
See Frances.

Frances:
From the Latin meaning "Frenchwoman" or possibly "free woman." *Alternative spellings:* Françoise, Francine, Paquita. *Short forms:* Fanny, Frankie, Frannie, Franny.

Francesca:
From the Italian meaning "French."

Francine:
See Frances.

Freda:
See Elfrida, Frederica, Frieda or Winifred.

Frederica:
The feminine form of Frederick (see Boys' Names). *Alternative spelling:* Frederique. *Short forms:* Froda, Froddie, Frida, Frieda, Fryda.

Freya:
From the Norse meaning "noble lady." *Alternative spellings:* Freja, Freyja, Froja.

Frida:
See Frieda.

Frieda:
From the Old German meaning "peace." *Alternative spellings:* Freda, Frida.

Fuchsia:
From the plant name.

G

Gabrielle:
From the Hebrew meaning "strong woman of God" or possibly "God is my strength." *Alternative spellings:* Gabriela, Gabriella. *Short forms:* Gabby, Gabbie, Gabi, Gaby, Gay.

Gail:
See Abigail.

Galilea:
From the Hebrew meaning "from Galilee."

Gemma:
From the Italian meaning "gem" or "precious stone." *Alternative spellings:* Germaine, Jemma.

Genesis:
From the Latin meaning "origin, birth."

Genevieve:
From the German meaning "fair one" or the Welsh meaning "fair," "white-browed," or "white wave." *Alternative spellings:* Gaynor, Guenevere, Guinevere, Gwendolyn, Jennifer. *Short forms:* Gena, Genna, Gennie, Genny, Gina, Jenni, Jennie, Jenny.

Georgeanne:
See Georgina.

Georgia:
See Georgina.

Georgiana:
See Georgina.

Georgina:
The feminine form of George (see Boys' Names). *Alternative spellings:* Georgeanne, Georgette, Georgia, Georgiana, Georgina, Georgine. *Short forms:* Geena, Georgie, Gigi, Gina, Ina.

Geraldine:
From the Old German meaning "spear ruler" or the Irish Gaelic meaning "one of the Fitzgeralds." *Short forms:* Geri, Gerry, Jerry.

Germaine:
From the French meaning "German"; see also Gemma. *Alternative spelling:* Jermaine.

Ghislaine:
From the French meaning "pledge" or "hostage." *Alternative spelling:* Ghislane.

Gia:
See Gianna.

Giada:
From the Italian meaning "jade."

Gianna:

The Italian feminine form of John. *Alternative spelling:* Giana. *Short form:* Gia.

Gigi:

From Gilberte.

Gilda:

From the English meaning "to gild."

Gillian:

A feminine form of Julian (see Boys' Names). *Alternative spellings:* Jillian, Juliana. *Short forms:* Gill, Gilly, Jill, Jilly.

Gina:

See Georgina and Regina.

Ginger:

See Virginia.

Ginny:

See Virginia.

Gioconda:

From the Italian origin, meaning "delight." *Alternative spellings:* Geoconda, Jeoconda.

Giovanna:

The Italian form of Jane.

Giselle:

From the Old German word *gisil,* meaning "pledge," or the Anglo-Saxon meaning "sword." *Alternative spellings:* Gisela, Gisèle, Gisell.

Gita:

From the Sanskrit meaning "song." *Alternative spelling:* Geeta.

Giulia:

See Julia.

Giuliana:

The Italian form of Julia. *Alternative spelling:* Giulia.

Gladys:

From the Welsh meaning "ruler" or possibly from the Latin meaning "a small sword." *Alternative spelling:* Gwladys. *Short forms:* Gladdie, Glads.

Glenda:

From the Welsh meaning "holy" or "good."

Glenys:

From the Welsh meaning "holy." *Alternative spellings:* Glenis, Glennis, Glennys.

G

Gloria:
From the Latin meaning "glory."
Alternative spellings: Glorianna, Glorianne, Glory.

Grace:
From the Latin meaning "thanks," "graceful," or "lovely."

Gracelyn:
A contemporary invented name. A blend of Grace and Lynn.

Gracie:
See Grace.

Graciela:
See Grace.

Gráinne:
From the Irish Gaelic meaning "love."

Greta:
See Margaret.

Gretchen:
See Margaret.

Griselda
From the German, meaning "dark battle." Also possibly "gray fighting maid."

Guadalupe:
Possibly from the Spanish meaning "wolf valley" or from the Arabic meaning "river of black stones." Also, "Our Lady of Guadalupe" was a Mexican Virgin Mary apparition of the 16th century.

Gwen:
From the Welsh meaning "white."

Gwendolyn:
See Genevieve. *Alternative spelling:* Gwendolen. *Short forms:* Gwen, Gwena, Gwenda, Gwendi, Gwinn, Gwynn, Wenda, Wendie, Wendoline, Wendy.

Gwyneth:
From the Welsh meaning "blessed." *Alternative spelling:* Gwynedd. *Short forms:* Gwen, Gwyn.

H

Hadley:
From the English meaning "heathery field."

Haley:
From the Old English *heg,* meaning "hay," and *leah,* meaning "clearing," or the Norse *haela,* meaning "hero." *Alternative spellings:* Haile, Hailee, Hailey, Hallie, Hayley.

Halle:
See Hallie.

Hallie:
From the Norse meaning "heroic." *Alternative spelling:* Halle.

Hannah:
From the Hebrew meaning "God has favored me." *Alternative spellings:* Hana, Hanna, Nancy.

Harley:
From the English meaning "long field."

Harmony:
From the Greek meaning "concord" or "in agreement." *Alternative spellings:* Harmonia, Harmonie.

Harper:
From the English meaning "Harp player."

Harriet:
See Henrietta. *Alternative spellings:* Harriette.

Haven:
From the English meaning "safe place."

Hayden:
From the English meaning "heather-grown hill."

Hayley:
See Haley.

Hazel:
From the English *haesel,* meaning "hazelnut."

Heather:
From the plant of the same name.

Heaven:
From the English meaning "place of beauty and happiness." Also from the Bible "where God and angels are said to dwell."

Heaven-Lee:
Origins for the use of this as a name are uncertain but it has suddenly begun to appear as a name. *Alternative spelling:* Heavenly.

H

Heidi:
From the Old German meaning "proud" or "noble."

Helen:
From the Greek *helios,* meaning "sun," or *elene,* meaning "bright one" or "light." *Alternative spellings:* Aileen, Ailie, Eileen, Eileigh, Elaine, Elana, Elane, Elanor, Elanora, Eleanor, Eleanore, Elen, Elena, Elenora, Elin, Elinor, Elle, Ellen, Elli, Ellie, Elly, Ellyn, Ellynn, Hela, Helaine, Heleen, Helena, Helene, Helina, Ilana, Ileanna, Ilena, Iliana, Ilona, Ilonka, Illuska, Lana, Leena, Leentje, Lena, Leni, Lenka, Lenore, Leona, Leonora, Leonore, Leora, Liana, Lina, Nell, Nelli, Nellie, Nelly, Nora, Olena, Olenka, Yelena.

Helena:
See Helen.

Helga:
From the Norse meaning "holy." *Alternative spellings:* Elga, Olga, Olenka.

Heloise:
See Louise. *Alternative spelling:* Eloise.

Henrietta:
The female form of Henry (See Boys' Names). *Short forms:* Harriet, Harry, Hattie, Hettie, Hetty.

Hera:
From the Greek meaning "queen" or "jealous."

Hermia:
From the Greek meaning "messenger."

Hermina:
From the Latin meaning "noble."

Hermione:
From the Greek meaning "earthly" or "messenger." *Alternative spellings:* Hermine, Herminia.

Hillary:
From the Latin *hilarius,* meaning "cheerful." *Alternative spellings:* Hilaire, Hilarie, Hilary.

Holly:
From the plant of the same name. *Alternative spelling:* Hollie.

Honor:
From the Latin meaning "acknowledgement," "recognition." *Alternative spellings:* Honey, Honora, Honoria, Horeen, Nora, Norah, Onora.

Hope:
From the Old English meaning "optimism."

Ianthe:

From the Greek meaning "violet flower."
Alternative spelling: Iolanthe.

Ida:

From the Old German *id,* meaning
"work," or the Old English meaning
"protection" or "possession." *Alternative
spellings:* Aida, Ide, Ita.

Idelle:

From the Welsh, meaning "bountiful."

Igrayne:

According to the legend, Igrayne was the
mother of King Arthur; the meaning is
unknown. *Alternative spellings:* Igraine,
Ygraine, Ygrayne.

Ilana:

From the Hebrew meaning "tree."
Alternative spelling: Ilona.

Iliana:

From the Greek meaning "from Ilium or
Troy." *Alternative spelling:* Ileana.

Ilona:

Possibly from the Hungarian meaning
"beauty"; see also Helen or Ilana.
Alternative spellings: Ilana, Ilonka. *Short
form:* Ili.

Ilse:

See Elizabeth.

Iman:

From the Arabic *iman,* meaning "faith" or
"belief," or *amana,* meaning "to believe."
Alternative spelling: Imani.

Imani:

From Arabic meaning "faith." See Iman.

Imelda:

From the Latin meaning "wishful."

Imogen:

Possibly from the Gaelic *inghean,*
meaning "girl" or "maiden," or the
Latin meaning "blameless," "innocent,"
"likeness," or "image." *Alternative
spellings:* Immogen, Imogene. *Short
forms:* Imo, Genie.

Ina:
See Georgina or Christina.

India:
After the sub continent. *Short form:* Indy.

Indiana:
After the American state. *Short form:* Indy.

Indira:
From the Sanskrit meaning "splendid." *Short form:* Indy.

Inez:
From the Spanish meaning "chaste." *Alternative spelling:* Ines.

Inga:
See Ingrid. *Alternative spelling:* Inge.

Inge:
Possibly from the Norse meaning "meadow"; see also Inga.

Ingrid:
From the Norwegian meaning "Ing's ride," Ing being the Norse god of fertility and crops who rode on a boar. *Alternative spelling:* Inga.

Innes:
From the Gaelic meaning "island."

Iolanthe:
See Ianthe.

Iona:
From the Scottish island in the Hebrides of the same name, possibly from the Old Norse meaning "island."

Ione:
Possibly from the Greek meaning "violet."

Ireland:
After the Country of that name.

Irene:
From the Greek *eirene,* meaning "peace." *Alternative spellings:* Eireen, Irina.

Iris:
From the Greek meaning "rainbow" or from the flower.

Irma:
From the German meaning "whole."

Isabel:
See Isabelle.

Isabella:
See Isabelle.

Isabelle:

See Elizabeth. *Alternative spellings:* Isabel, Isabela, Isabell, Isabella, Izabella, Izabelle. *Short forms:* Bella, Isa, Issi, Issie, Issy, Sabelle.

Isadora:

From the Greek meaning "gift of Iris." *Alternative spelling:* Isidora.

Isis:

From the Egyptian meaning "supreme Goddess."

Isla:

From the Scottish island Islay. *Alternative spelling:* Ila.

Isobel:

See Isabelle.

Isola:

From the Latin meaning "isolated" or "alone."

Itzel:

From the Spanish meaning "protected."

Ivy:

From the plant of the same name.

Iyana:

From the Slavic meaning "God is gracious." Feminine form of Ivan.

Izabelle:

See Isabelle.

J

Jacey:
A contemporary invented name. A blend of J and C. *Alternative spelling:* Jaycee.

Jaclyn:
See Jacqueline.

Jacqueline:
A feminine form of James (see Boys' Names). *Alternative spellings:* Jacaline, Jackalyn, Jacquelyn, Jacquetta. Jaqueline. *Short forms:* Jackey, Jacki, Jackie, Jacksey, Jacksie, Jacky, Jacqui.

Jada:
The Spanish form of Jade. *Alternative spellings:* Jaida, Jayda.

Jade:
From the Latin meaning "fierce" or from the precious stone. *Alternative spelling:* Jayde.

Jaden:
A contemporary invented name. A blend of Jay and Aiden. *Alternative spellings:* Jadyn, Jaiden, Jaidyn, Jayden.

Jaeda:
From the Arabic for "goodness."

Jaelyn:
See Jaylynn. *Alternative spelling:* Jaelynn.

Jaida:
See Jada.

Jakayla:
A contemporary invented name. A blend of Jaqueline and Makayla.

Jalila:
From the Arabic meaning "great" or "illustrious."

Jaliyah:
Of contemporary origin. An invented name based on the name Aliyah.

Jamie:
A feminine form of James (see Boys' Names).

Jamilah:
From the Arabic meaning "beautiful" or "elegant." *Alternative spelling:* Jamila.

Jamya:
A contemporary invented name. A blend of Jamie and Tanya.

Jan:
See Janet.

Jana:
See Jane.

Janae:
See Jane.

Jane:
Feminine form of John (see Boys' Names). *Alternative spellings:* Ivana, Jan, Jana, Janae, Janean, Janeen, Janel, Janela, Janella, Janelle, Janessa, Janet, Janeta, Janetta, Janette, Janey, Janka, Jani, Janica, Janice, Janie, Janina, Janine, Janis, Janita, Janith, Janna, Jannelle, Jany, Jayne, Jaynie, Jean, Jeanne, Jeanette, Jeani, Jeanie, Jeanine, Jehane, Jene, Jenni, Jennie, Jenny, Jess, Jessi, Jessie, Jessy, Jinni, Jinnie, Jinny, Joan, Joanna, Joanne, Joeann, Johanna, Joni, Jonie, Jony, Jovanna, Seonaid, Sheena, Sian, Sinéad, Siobhán.

Janelle:
A combination of Jane and Danielle.

Janessa:
A combination of Jane and Vanessa.

Janet:
A Scottish form of Jane derived from the French form Jeannette. *Alternative spellings:* Jan, Janella, Janelle, Janete, Janetta, Janette, Janot, Netta, Nettie, Seonaid.

Janiah:
See Janiya.

Janice:
See Jane.

Janis:
See Jane.

Janiya:
Of contemporary origin. An invented name based on the name Jane. *Alternative spelling:* Janiah, Janiyah.

Jaslene:
See Jocelyn.

Jasmin:
From the Persian or Arabic yasmin, meaning "an olive flower." *Alternative spellings:* Jasmina, Jasmine, Jasmyn, Jazmine, Jazmyn, Jesmond, Jessamine, Jessamy, Jessie, Yasmin, Yasmina, Yasmine.

Jaycee:
See Jacey.

Jayda:
See Jada.

Jayden:
See Jaden.

J

Jayla:
A contemporary invented name. A blend of Jada and Kayla. *Alternative spelling:* Jaylah.

Jaylee:
See Jaylynn.

Jaylynn:
A contemporary invented name. A blend of Jay and Lynn. *Alternative spellings:* Jaelyn, Jaelynn, Jailyn, Jalynn, Jaylee, Jayleen, Jaylen, Jaylene, Jaylin, Jaylyn.

Jazlyn:
A contemporary invented name. A blend of Jaz and Lynn. *Alternative spelling:* Jazlynn.

Jazmin:
See Jasmin. *Alternative spelling:* Jazmine, Jazmyn.

Jean:
See Jane. *Short forms:* Jeni, Jenny, Gene, Genie, Jeane, Jeanie, Jeanne, Jeannine.

Jeanette:
French form of Jean. *Alternative spelling:* Jeannette.

Jeanine:
From the Old French name Jehanne, a form of Jane.

Jemima:
From the Hebrew meaning "dove." *Alternative spelling:* Jemimah. *Short forms:* Jem, Jemma, Mima.

Jemma:
See Gemma or Jemima.

Jenna:
Possibly from Jennifer.

Jennifer:
From the Celtic meaning "fair" and "yielding." Possibly also from the names Guenevere, Genevieve, or Gwendolyn. *Alternative spellings:* Jenfer, Jenifer. *Short forms:* Jen, Jeni, Jennie, Jenny, Jinny.

Jermaine:
See Germaine.

girls' names

Jessica:
From the Hebrew meaning "he beholds" or "the rich one." *Alternative spellings:* Jesika, Jessika. *Short forms:* Jess, Jessie, Jessy, Jessye.

Jessie:
From the Hebrew *yishai,* meaning "riches" or "a gift"; see also Jessica. *Alternative spellings:* Jessi, Jessey.

Jet:
From the French *jaiet,* meaning "black gem stone." *Alternative spelling:* Jetta.

Jewel:
From the French meaning "gemstone." *Alternative spelling:* Jewell.

Jillian:
See Gillian. *Short form:* Jilly, Jill.

Jimena:
See Ximena.

Jinny:
See Virginia.

Joan:
See Jane. *Alternative spellings:* Henise, Janis, Janna, Jean, Joana, Joann, Joanne, Joeann, Johan, Johna, Jonet, Joni, Jonie, Jovana, Juana, Juanita.

Joana:
See Joan. *Alternative spellings:* Joane, Joanna, Jo-Anne, Joanne, Joanna.

Jocelyn:
From the Latin meaning "cheerful" or "sportive" or the Celtic name Josse, meaning "champion." *Alternative spellings:* Jaslene, Jocelin, Joceline, Jocelyn, Jocelyne, Joscelin, Joscelind, Josceline, Joselin, Josette, Joslyn. *Short forms:* Jo, Joey, Josie, Josey.

Jodie:
See Judith. *Alternative spelling:* Jodi, Jody.

Johanna:
See Jane. *Alternative spelling:* Johana.

Jolie:
From the French meaning "pretty one."

Jordan:
From the Hebrew meaning "flowing down." *Alternative spellings:* Jordain, Jordaine, Jordann, Jorden, Jordin, Jordyn.

Josephine:
A feminine form of Joseph (see Boys' Names). *Alternative spelling:* Josephina. *Short forms:* Fifi, Jo, Joey, Josette, Josie, Posey.

Josie:
See Jocelyn or Josephine.

Journey:
From the English meaning "travel, journey."

Joy:
From the Latin *jocosa,* meaning "merry."

Joyce:
From the Latin meaning "joyous" or the English meaning "cheerful" or "merry." *Alternative spellings:* Joice, Joisse. *Short forms:* Joy, Josie, Jo.

Juanita:
See Joan. *Short form:* Nita.

Judith:
From the Hebrew meaning "praised." *Alternative spelling:* Judit. *Short forms:* Jodie, Judi, Judie, Judy.

Julia:
A feminine form of Julian (see Boys' Names). *Alternative spellings:* Gillian, Gillie, Giulia, Juillia, Julca, Julcia, Juli, Juliana, Juliane, Julianna, Julie, Juliet, Julieta, Julietta, Julina, Juline, Julinka, Juliska, Julissa, Julita, Julka. *Short forms:* Jul, Jula, Julie.

Juliana:
See Julia. *Alternative spellings:* Julianna, Julianne.

Julie:
A French form of Julia.

Juliet:
See Julia. *Alternative spellings:* Juliette, Julietta, Jullietta, Julliette.

Julissa:
A contemporary invented name. A blend of Julia and Alissa.

June:
From the month or from the Latin *juvenior,* meaning "young."

Juniper:
From the plant.

Juno:
From the Latin meaning "queen."

Justice:
From the Latin meaning "righteous, just, fair."

Justine:
From the Latin meaning "just."

K

Kadence:
See Kaydence.

Kaela:
From the Hebrew or Arabic meaning "beloved sweetheart."

Kaelyn:
See Kaylynn.

Kaia:
From the Greek meaning "Earth."

Kaila:
From the Hebrew meaning "laurel crown." *Alternative spellings:* Kallie, Kayla.

Kailyn:
See Kaylynn

Kaitlin:
See Catherine. *Alternative spellings:* Caitlin, Kaitlyn, Kaitlynn.

Kaiya:
From the Japanese meaning "forgiveness."

Kaley:
See Kay. *Alternative spellings:* Kailee, Kailey, Kaylee, Kayleigh, Kayley, kaylie.

Kali:
From the Sanskrit meaning "black one." *Alternative spelling:* Kallie.

Kaliyah:
Of contemporary origin. An invented name based on Aliyah.

Kallie:
See Kaila.

Kallista:
From the Greek meaning "beautiful." *Alternative spelling:* Callista.

Kameron:
See Cameron.

Kamila:
See Camilla.

Kamryn:
See Cameron.

Kara:
See Catherine.

Karen:
See Catherine. *Alternative spellings:* Caryn, Karan, Karin, Karina, Karon, Karren, Karrin, Karyn, Keren, Koren.

K

K

Karesa:
See Catherine.

Karina:
See Carina.

Karis:
From the Greek meaning "grace."

Karisma:
From the Greek meaning "favor" or "grace."

Karissa:
See Carissa.

Karla:
See Carla.

Karlie:
See Carla. *Alternative spellings:* Karlee, Karley, Karli, Karlie.

Karma:
From the Hindi meaning "fate, destiny."

Karrie:
See Caroline. *Alternative spelling:* Kari.

Kasey:
See Casey.

Kassady:
See Cassidy. *Alternative spellings:* Cassady, Kassidy.

Kassandra:
See Cassandra.

Kassidy:
See Cassidy.

Kate:
See Catherine.

Katelyn:
A contemporary invented name. A blend of Kate and Lynn. *Alternative spellings:* Katelynn, Katlyn.

Katherine:
See Catherine.

Kathleen:
See Caitlin or Catherine. *Alternative spellings:* Kathleena, Kathlena, Kathlene, Kathlyn, Kathlynn.

Kathy:
See Catherine.

Katie:
See Catherine. *Alternative spellings:* Kat, Kata, Kate, Katee, Katey, Kati, Katia, Katianne, Katinka, Katt, Katy, Katya.

Katrina:
See Catherine. *Alternative spellings:* Katrin, Katrine. *Short form:* Trina.

Kay:
From the English or Scandinavian meaning "keeper of the keys." *Alternative spellings:* Cayla, Kayla, Kayloo.

Kaya:
From the Native American Hopi meaning "my elder sister" or "wise child."

Kayden:
A contemporary invented name. A blend of Kay and Denise. Possibly a short form of Kaydence.

Kaydence:
See Cadence. *Short form:* Kayden.

Kayla:
From the Arabic and Hebrew meaning "laurel, crown." *Alternative spellings:* Kaylah, Keyla.

Kaylah:
See Kayla.

Kaylee:
A contemporary invented name. A blend of Kay and Lee. *Alternative spellings:* Kailey, Kailyn.

Kaylin:
See Kaylynn.

Kaylynn:
A contemporary invented name. A blend of Kay and Lynn. *Alternative spellings:* Kaelyn, Kailyn, Kaylin, Kaylyn.

Keegan:
From the Irish Gaelic meaning "little fierce one."

Keely:
From the Irish Gaelic meaning "good-looking," "lively," or "aggressive."

Keira:
A form of Kiara.

Kelis:
A contemporary invented name.

Kelly:
From the Irish meaning "lively" or "aggressive." *Alternative spellings:* Kelley, Kelleigh, Kelli.

Kelsey:
From the English meaning "island." *Alternative spelling:* Kelsie.

K

Kendall:
From the English meaning "ruler of the valley." *Alternative spelling:* Kendal.

Kendra:
From the Old English meaning "wise" or "all-knowing." *Alternative spelling:* Kindra.

Kenia:
See Kenya.

Kenna:
The feminine form of Kenneth.

Kennedy:
From the Irish meaning "helmeted chief." *Alternative spelling:* Kennedi.

Kenya:
From the country in Africa. *Alternative spelling:* Kenia.

Kenzie:
See Mackenzie.

Kerby:
See Kirby.

Keren:
From the Hebrew meaning "beauty"; see also Karen. *Alternative spellings:* Kerrin, Keryn.

Kerensa:
From the English *cres,* meaning "peace" and "love."

Kerry:
From the Irish Gaelic meaning "dusky" or "dark." *Alternative spellings:* Kerri, Kerrie.

Keyla:
See Kayla.

Kezia:
From the Hebrew meaning "sweet smelling spice." *Alternative spelling:* Keziah. *Short form:* Kezzie.

Khayla:
See Michaela.

Khloe:
See Chloe.

Kianna:
A contemporary invented name. A blend of Ki and Anna. *Alternative spelling:* Kiana.

Kiara:
See Ciara. *Alternative spellings:* Kiera, Kira.

Kiera:

The feminine form of Kieran (see Boys' Names). *Alternative spellings:* Ciara, Ciera, Keara, Keira, Kieran, Kierran.

Kiersten:

See Kirstin.

Kiley:

See Kylie.

Kim:

From the Old English meaning "royally born." *Alternative spelling:* Kym.

Kimberly:

From the Old English meaning "king's wood." *Alternative spellings:* Kimberlee, Kimberleigh, Kimberley, Kimberli, Kymberlie, Kimberlin, Kimberlyn, Kymberley.

Kimora:

A contemporary invented name. A blend of Kim and Nora.

Kindra:

See Kendra.

Kinsey:

From the Old Norse *kyn,* meaning "family."

Kinsley:

From the English meaning "King's meadow." *Alternative spelling:* Kinley.

Kira:

From Greek *cyrus,* meaning "sun," or the Russian meaning "lady"; see also Ciara.

Kirby:

From the English meaning "church farm." *Alternative spelling:* Kerby

Kirstin:

See Christina. *Alternative spellings:* Kerstin, Kiersten, Kierstin, Kierston, Kirsten, Kirstine, Kirstyn, Kyrstin.

Kirsty:

See Christina.

Kitty:

See Katherine.

Klarissa:

See Clarissa.

Konstance:

See Constance.

Kora:

See Cora.

K

Korina:

See Corinne. *Alternative spelling:* Corrina.

Krista:

The Czech form of Christina.

Kristen:

See Christina.

Kristi:

See Christina.

Kristin:

See Christine.

Kristina:

See Christina.

Krystal:

From the Greek *krystallos,* meaning "ice"; see also Crystal. *Alternative spelling:* Krystle.

Kyla:

From the Gaelic *caol,* meaning "narrow." *Alternative spelling:* Kylah.

Kyle:

From the Gaelic Irish meaning "narrow strip of land" or the Yiddish meaning "crowned with laurel."

Kylie:

From the Aboriginal meaning "curved stick" (boomerang). *Alternative spellings:* Kylee, Kyleigh.

Kyra:

From the Greek meaning "lady."

Kyria:

From the Greek meaning "lord" or "god."

Lacey:
From the English meaning "lace." *Alternative spellings:* Laci, Lacy.

Laila:
From the Persian meaning "night" or "dark-haired." *Alternative spellings:* Laili, Laleh, Layla, Leyla.

Lana:
See Alana.

Laney:
A contemporary invented name. A blend of Lacey and Lindsay. *Alternative spelling:* Lainey.

Lani:
From the Hawaiian meaning "sky."

Lara:
From the Latin meaning "famous" or "protection"; see also Larissa.

Larissa:
From the Greek meaning "cheerful" or "playfulness." *Alternative spellings:* Laris, Larisa, Lissa. *Short form:* Lara.

Laura:
From the Latin meaning "laurel." *Alternative spellings:* Laurie, Loretta.

Laurel:
From the Greek meaning "strength" or "courage" or the English meaning "laurel tree." *Alternative spelling:* Lorel.

Lauren:
From the Latin *lawrentium,* meaning "the place of the laurel trees" or "laurel crowned." *Alternative spellings:* Lauryn, Loren, Lorena.

Layla:
See Laila or Lila. *Alternative spelling:* Leyla.

Lea:
From the Old English meaning "field" or "meadow." *Alternative spelling:* Lee, Leigh.

Leah:
From the Hebrew meaning "weak eyes" or "languid." *Alternative spellings:* Lea, Lee, Leia, Leigh, Lia.

Leandra:
From the Greek meaning "lioness."

Leanna:
See Lianne.

Leanora:
See Eleanor.

L

Lee:
From the Irish meaning "poetic" or the Chinese meaning "plum"; see also Lea, Leah. *Alternative spelling:* Leigh.

Leena:
From the Sanskrit meaning "devoted"; see also Helen. *Alternative spelling:* Lena.

Leia:
See Leah.

Leila:
From the Persian meaning "night." *Alternative spellings:* Leilah, Lila.

Leilani:
From the Hawaiian *lani,* meaning "heavenly" or "of the sky," and *lei,* meaning "flower," thus "heavenly flower."

Lena:
Originally as a name ending of names such as Helena and Marlene. Used as an independent name since the mid-19th century. *Alternative spellings:* Lina.

Leonie:
From the Greek *leon* or the Latin *leo,* meaning "lion." *Alternative spellings:* Leona, Leontine, Leontina. *Short form:* Leo.

Lesley:
Female version of Leslie (see Boys' Names). *Alternative spellings:* Leslee, Leslie, Lesly. *Short form:* Lee.

Leticia:
From the Latin meaning "gladness" or "joyfulness." *Alternative spellings:* Laeticia, Laetitia, Letitia. *Short forms:* Laeta, Letty, Tia, Tisha.

Lexie:
See Alexandra. *Alternative spelling:* Lexi.

Leyla:
See Layla.

Lia:
From the Greek meaning "bringer of good news." See also Leah.

Liana:
From the Latin for "young" and the French meaning "to climb like a vine."

Lianne:
From the Greek *helios,* meaning "sun"; the Latin meaning "youth"; or the English meaning "meadow." *Alternative spellings:* Leanne, Lian, Liana, Liane, Lianna.

Libby:
See Elizabeth.

Liberty:
From the Latin meaning "free."

Liesel:
See Elizabeth. *Alternative spelling:* Liesl.

Lila:
From the Hebrew meaning "night."
Alternative spellings: Lilah, Liliah, Layla,
Laylah.

Lilia:
From the Latin meaning "lilies."

Lilian:
From the Latin meaning "lily." *Alternative
spelling:* Lillian. Short form: Lily.

Liliana:
The Italian and Spanish form of Lilian.
Alternative spellings: Lilianna, Lilliana,
Lillianna, Lilyana.

Lilith:
From the Arabic meaning "of the night."

Lily:
See Lilian. *Alternative spellings:* Lillie,
Lilly.

Lina:
See Lena.

Linda:
Possibly from the German meaning
"linden tree"; possibly the Spanish *linda,*
meaning "pretty"; or possibly a short
form of names ending in -lind , meaning
"weak," "tender," or "soft." *Short forms:*
Lin, Lyn.

Lindsay:
(See Boys' Names.) *Alternative
spellings:* Lindsey, Linsey, Lynsey.

Lisa:
From the French meaning "blessed" or
"gifted"; see also Elizabeth.

Lisanne:
Combination of Lisa and Anne.

Lisette:
See Elizabeth.

Litzy:
A contemporary invented name. The
name of a Mexican pop singer.

Livia:
See Olivia.

L

Liza:
See Elizabeth.

Lizbeth:
See Elizabeth.

Lizeth:
See Elizabeth.

Logan:
From the Scottish meaning "low meadow" or possibly after the Scottish place of the same name in Ayrshire.

Lois:
From the Greek meaning "good" or "desirable."

Lola:
See Carlotta, Dolores, or Louise.

Lolita:
See Dolores.

London:
From the English "fortress of the moon." The capital city of the United Kingdom. *Alternative spelling:* Londyn.

Loni:
See Alona.

Lonita:
From the Spanish meaning "little one."

Lorelei:
From the German meaning "song" or "alluring."

Lorena:
See Lauren.

Loretta:
See Laura. *Alternative spelling:* Lauretta.

Lorna:
From the Scottish place name. *Alternative spellings:* Lorne, Lorn.

Lorraine:
From the Latin meaning "full of sorrow" or from the French region. *Alternative spellings:* Laraine, Loraine. *Short form:* Lori.

Lottie:
See Charlotte.

Lotty:
See Charlotte.

Louisa:
From the French meaning "famous." *Short form:* Lulu.

Louise:
From the French meaning "famous."
Short forms: Lola, Lou, Louie, Louella, Luella.

Lucero:
From the Latin meaning "lamp, circle of light."

Lucia:
The Italian and Spanish form of Lucy.
Alternative spellings: Luciana.

Luciana:
See Lucia.

Lucille:
See Lucy.

Lucinda:
From the Latin meaning "light." *Short form:* Cindy.

Lucretia:
Female version of the Roman family name Lucretius, possibly from the Latin meaning "rich" or "rewarded."
Alternative spelling: Lucrezia.

Lucy:
From the Latin meaning "light."

Ludmilla:
From the Slav meaning "people" and "grace."

Luella:
See Louise.

Luna:
From the Latin meaning "moon."

Luz:
From the Spanish meaning "light."

L

Lydia:
From the Greek meaning "a native of Lydia," an ancient city in Aisa Minor.

Lyla:
From the French meaning "island."

Lyn:
Possibly from the Old English meaning "dweller by the waterfall"; see also Linda. *Alternative spellings:* Lin, Lina, Linn, Linne, Lynette, Lynn.

Lyric:
From the Greek *lurikos,* meaning "to express thoughts or feelings."

M

Mackenzie:
From the Irish meaning "child of the wise leader." *Alternative spellings:* Makena, Makenna, Makenzie, Mckenzie. *Short form:* Kenzie.

Macy:
Possibly from the Old French meaning "weapon" or English for "Matthew's estate." *Alternative spellings:* Macey, Maci, Macie.

Maddy:
See Madeleine.

Madeline:
The French form of Magdalen. *Alternative spellings:* Madaleine, Madaline, Madalyn, Madelaine, Madeleine, Madelin, Madelina, Madella. *Short forms:* Maddy, Madge, Mads, Laine.

Madison:
Possibly from Magdalen; from the American surname or the Old English meaning "son of Maud." *Alternative spellings:* Maddison, Madisyn, Madyson. *Short forms:* Maddy, Maddie.

Madonna:
From the Italian name for the Virgin Mary or the Italian meaning "my Lady." *Short forms:* Maddy, Madge, Maddie, Mads.

Maeve:
From the Irish Gaelic *meadhbh,* meaning "intoxicating" or "joyous"; see also Mavis. *Alternative spellings:* Maive, Mave, Meave, Meaveen.

Magdalen:
See Magdalena.

Magdalena:
From the Greek meaning "high tower." *Alternative spellings:* Madigan, Magdalina, Magdelana, Magdalene. *Short forms:* Magda, Malena.

Maggie:
From the Hebrew meaning "pearl"; see Magdalene, Margaret.

Maia:
See Maya.

Makayla:
See Michaela. *Alternative spelling:* Makaila.

Makena:
See Makenzie.

Makenzie:
See Mackenzie.

Maleah:
See Malia

Malena:
See Magdalena. *Alternative spelling:* Malina.

Malia:
The Hawaiian form of Mary. *Alternative spellings:* Maleah, Maliyah.

Maliha:
From the Arabic meaning "nice" or "good."

Mallory:
From the French meaning "unfortunate" or possibly from the Old German meaning "an army counsellor." *Alternative spellings:* Mallary, Malerie, Mallery, Malloree, Mallorey, Mellory. *Short forms:* Mallie, Mally.

Mandy:
From the Latin meaning "loved"; see also Amanda. *Alternative spellings:* Mandi, Mandee, Mandie

Mara:
From the Hebrew meaning "bitter"; see Mary.

Marely:
See Marley.

Maren:
From the Latin meaning "sea." Also the Aramaic form of Mary.

M

Margaret:
From the Hebrew *margaron,* meaning "pearl." *Alternative spellings:* Margarita, Margery, Margot, Marguerite, Marquette. Mereid. *Short forms:* Daisy, Greta, Gretchen, Madge, Maggie, Mags, Maisie, Mamie, Margo, Margot, Meg, Megan, Meggie, Mog, Peg, Pegeen, Peggy, Polly, Rita.

Margarita:
From the Spanish meaning "daisy." *Alternative spellings:* Margaux, Margo, Margot, Marquerita.

Margaux:
See Margarita. *Alternative spellings:* Margot, Margo.

M

Maria:
See Mary. *Short forms:* Mimi, Ria.

Mariah:
See Mary.

Mariam:
From the Hebrew meaning either "sea of bitterness" or "child of our wishes"; See also Mary.

Marian:
See Mary. *Alternative spellings:* Marianne, Maryanne.

Mariana:
See Mary. *Alternative spelling:* Marianna.

Maribel:
From the French meaning "beautiful Mary." *Alternative spellings:* Marabel, Marbelle, Maribell, Maribella, Maribelle.

Marie:
See Mary.

Mariela:
See Mary. *Alternative spelling:* Mariella.

Marieta:
From the Italian meaning "grace and beauty." *Alternative spellings:* Maretta, Marietta, Marrietta.

Marilyn:
Possibly from Mary meaning "Mary's line" or possibly a blend of Mary and Ellen or Lynn. *Alternative spellings:* Maralyn, Marlyn, Marilynn, Marylyn.

Marina:
From the Latin meaning "of the sea." *Alternative spellings:* Mare, Maris, Marisa, Marissa, Marne, Marni, Marnie, Marnina, Marys, Rina.

Marion:
See Mary.

Marisa:
From the Latin meaning "a gem," "a special one," or "of the sea." *Alternative spellings:* Marijse, Marissa. *Short form:* Marie.

Marisol:
From the Spanish meaning "sea and sun."

Maritza:
From the Arabic meaning "blessed."

Mariyah:
A form of Maria.

Marla:
See Marlene.

Marlee:
See Marley.

Marlen:
See Marlene.

Marlene:
See Magdalena.

Marley:
From the English meaning "pleasant seaside meadow." *Alternative spellings:* Marely, Marlee.

Martha:
From the Aramaic meaning "lady." *Alternative spellings:* Marta, Martelle, Marthe, Mattie, Matty.

Martina:
From the Latin meaning "martial" or "warlike." *Alternative spellings:* Martelle, Martine, Martino. *Short forms:* Marta, Marti, Marty.

Martine:
See Martina. *Short form:* Marti, Marty.

Marvel:
From the Latin meaning "full of wonder." *Alternative spellings:* Marvell, Marvella, Marvelle.

Mary:
From the Hebrew name Miriam, meaning "sea of bitterness" or "O child of our wishes," or the Latin *stella maris,* meaning "star of the sea." *Alternative spellings:* Mair, Maire, Mairi, Mairin, Mame, Mamie, Manon, Mara, Marabel, Marella, Mari, Maria, Mariah, Mariam, Marian, Mariana, Marianna, Maribel, Marice, Marie, Mariel, Marietta, Mariette, Marilee, Marilin, Marilla, Marilyn, Marion, Marita, Marlo, Marlyse, Marren, Marya, Maryam, Maryann, Maryanna, Maryanne, Marylin, Marylinn, Marylyn, Maura, Maureen, Maurene, Maurie, May, Meirion, Meri, Meriel, Merrill, Meryl, Mia, Millie, Mimi, Minette, Minni, Minnie, Minny, Miriam, Moira, Molly, Muriel, Muriell, Polli, Pollie, Polly.

Maryam:
See Miriam.

Maryjane:
A contemporary invented name. A blend of Mary and Jane.

Matilda:
From the Old German meaning "mighty in battle." *Alternative spellings:* Mathilda, Maud. *Short forms:* Matti, Mattie, Matty, Tilda, Tilly.

M

M

Mattie:
See Martha.

Maureen:
A Gaelic version of *Mairin,* derived from Mary, possibly meaning "little Mary" or "little bitter one," or the French meaning "dark-skinned." *Alternative spelling:* Moreen. *Short form:* Mo.

Maxine:
From the Latin meaning "greatest." *Alternative spellings:* Maxeene, Maxene, Maxina. *Short forms:* Maxie, Maxy.

May:
From the Latin *Maius,* meaning "the month of May." *Alternative spellings:* Mae, Mai

Maya:
From the Latin *mai,* meaning "I greet"; after the Roman goddess Maia, the mother of Mercury; the Sanskrit meaning "illusion"; or the Greek meaning "great." *Alternative spelling:* Maia.

Mayra:
From the Australian meaning "spring wind."

Mckayla:
See Michaela

Mckenna:
See Mackenzie.

Mckenzie:
See Mackenzie.

Meadow:
From the English meaning "meadow; a grassy field."

Megan:
The Welsh form of Margaret. *Alternative spellings:* Maegan, Meghan, Meghann, Meighen.

Melanie:
From the Greek meaning "black" or "dark complexion." *Alternative spellings:* Melaine, Melana, Melanee, Melonie. *Short form:* Mel.

Melantha:
From the Greek meaning "dark flower."

Melina:
From the Greek meaning "honey."

Melinda:
See Melissa. *Short form:* Mindy.

Meliora:
From the Latin meaning "better."

Melisande:
See Melissa.

Melissa:
From the Greek meaning "honey bee" or the Gaelic name Maoiliosa, meaning "of which is sweet Jesus." *Alternative spellings:* Malesa, Melessa, Melinda, Melita, Melitta, Melisande, Missy.

Melody:
From the Greek meaning "song" or "music." *Alternative spellings:* Melodi, Melodie.

Melora:
From the Greek meaning "golden melon" or "golden apple."

Melvina:
The feminine form of Melvin (see Boys' Names).

Mena:
From the Dutch or German meaning "strong"; see also Philomena.

Mercedes:
From the Spanish name for the Virgin Mary meaning "Our Lady of Mercies" or the Spanish meaning "merciful." *Short form:* Mercy.

Mercer:
From the Old English meaning "merchant."

Mercia:
See Mercy.

Mercy:
From the Latin *merces,* meaning "reward"; see also Mercedes. *Alternative spellings:* Mercia, Merilee.

Meredith:
Possibly from the Welsh Meredudd, meaning "pretty," "Lord," or possibly "from the sea." *Alternative spellings:* Meredithe, Meridith. *Short form:* Merry.

M

Mererid:
Welsh version of Margaret.

Meri:
From the Finnish meaning "the ocean" or "the sea" or the Hebrew meaning "rebellious."

Meriel:
From the Gaelic Irish meaning "shining sea."

Merilee:
See Mercy. *Alternative spelling:* Merrily.

M

Merle:
From the French meaning "blackbird." *Alternative spellings:* Meril, Merrill, Merla.

Merlin:
See Boys' Names.

Merrill:
See Mary, Merle or Muriel.

Meryl:
See Muriel.

Mia:
From the Italian meaning "my"; see also Mary. *Alternative spelling:* Miah.

Micah:
A feminine form of Michael (see Boys' Names). *Alternative spellings:* Mika, Mycah.

Michaela:
A feminine form of Michael (see Boys' Names). *Alternative spellings:* Micaela, Michal, Michala, Michelle, Mikaeli. *Short form:* Khayla.

Michal:
See Michaela. *Alternative spellings:* Michael, Mikal.

Michelle:
See Michaela. *Alternative spellings:* Michell, Michella, Mishell, Mishelle. *Short forms:* Shelly, Shelley.

Mila:
From the Russian meaning "dear one."

Mildred:
From the Old English meaning "gentle strength." *Short form:* Mil, Milda, Millie, Milly, Mindy.

Miley:
A contemporary invented name, from the nickname "Smiley" of singer/actress Miley Cyrus. *Alternative spellings:* Mylee, Mylie.

Milla:
See Camilla.

Millicent:
From the Old German meaning "strength" or "work." *Alternative spellings:* Melicent, Melita, Melieta. *Short forms:* Millie, Milly.

Millie:
See Millicent.

Mima:
See Jemima.

Mimi:
See Maria.

Mimosa:
From the Latin meaning "imitative" or the flower.

Mina:
From the Old German meaning "love"; the Hindi meaning "blue sky"; or the Arabic meaning "harbor." *Alternative spellings:* Minee, Minna, Minnie, Minny.

Mindy:
See Melinda.

Minerva:
From the Latin meaning "wise." *Short form:* Minnie, Minny.

Minnie:
See Mina, Minerva, or Wilhemina. *Alternative spelling:* Minny.

Mira:
From the Spanish meaning "look"; see also Mirabel.

Mirabel:
From the Latin meaning "wonderful." *Alternative spellings:* Mirabella, Mirabelle. *Short form:* Mira.

Miracle:
From the Latin meaning "wonder, marvel."

Miranda:
Possibly from the Latin *mirari,* meaning "admirable" or "lovely," or the Latin *mirandus,* meaning "astonished" or "amazed."

Miriam:
From the Hebrew name Maryam, linked to Mary, meaning "star of the sea."

Misty:
From the Old English meaning "clouded" or "obscured."

Mitra:
From the Persian meaning "bright," as in bright sun.

Miya:
From the Japanese meaning "temple."

Mo:
See Maureen.

Moira:
Gaelic Irish meaning "great"; see also Mary. *Alternative spellings:* Moyra, Myra.

Molly:
See Mary. *Alternative spelling:* Mollie.

M

Mona:
From the Gaelic Irish meaning "noble" or "nun," "sweet angel"; possibly the Greek meaning "single"; the Arabic meaning "wish," or the Old English meaning "month."

Monica:
From the Latin meaning "advisor." *Alternative spellings: Mona, Monika, Monique.*

Monique:
See Monica.

Monserrat:
From the Catalan meaning "serrated mountain."

Montana:
From the Latin meaning "mountain" or from the state.

Mor:
From the Gaelic meaning "great, large."

Mora:
From the Gaelic meaning "the sun."

Morag:
From the Gaelic meaning "great" or possibly "the sun."

Morgan:
From the Old Welsh meaning "sea shore" or "bright sea."

Moriah:
From the Hebrew meaning "god is my teacher."

Morna:
From the Gaelic meaning "beloved."

Muriel:
From the Irish meaning "bright sea"; see also Mary. *Alternative spellings: Meriel, Merril, Merrill, Merryl, Meryl, Miriel, Murial.*

Mya:
From the Burmese meaning "emerald." *Alternative spelling: Myah.*

Myla:
From the English meaning "merciful."

Mylee:
See Miley.

Myra:
See Moira. *Alternative spelling: Mira.*

N

Naamah:
From the Hebrew meaning "loved," "beautiful," or "pleasant." *Alternative spelling:* Naama.

Nabila:
From the Arabic meaning "noble."

Nadean:
From the Russian *Nadezhda,* meaning "hope." *Alternative spelling:* Nadine.

Nadia:
From the Russian meaning "hope." *Alternative spellings:* Nadja, Nadya.

Nadimah:
From the Arabic meaning "friend."

Naia:
From the Greek *naein,* meaning "to flow."

Naima:
From the Arabic meaning "comfortable" or "tranquil." *Alternative spelling:* Naeema.

Nairne:
From the Scottish Gaelic meaning "riverside of lime trees."

Nan:
See Anne, Nanette, or Nancy.

Nana:
See Anne or Nanette.

Nancy:
See Anne or Hannah. *Alternative spellings:* Nancey, Nanci, Nancie. *Short forms:* Nan, Nann.

Nanette:
From the Hebrew meaning "grace" or "God has been gracious." *Short forms:* Nan, Nana, Netty.

Naomi:
From the Hebrew or Arabic meaning "pleasant" or "pleasantness." *Alternative spellings:* Naima, Neema, Noemi, Noemie.

Nara:
From the Celtic meaning "happy" or the Old English meaning "one who is near or dear."

Narcissa:
From the Greek *narke,* meaning "numbness," or possibly meaning "daffodil." *Alternative spellings:* Narcisa, Narcisse.

Nariko:
From the Japanese meaning "gentle child."

N

Nastasia:
See Anastasia.

Natalia:
The Russian form of Natalie.

Natalie:
From the Latin *natalis dies,* meaning "birthday." *Alternative spellings:* Natalee, Natalia, Nataly, Natalya, Natasha, Nathalie, Nathalee, Nathalia, Nathaly. *Short forms:* Nat, Talya.

Natalya:
The Russian form of Natalia.

Natasha:
See Natalie. *Alternative spellings:* Natacha, Natacia, Natasa, Natashea, Natashia, Natashja, Natashka, Natisha. *Short forms:* Stacey, Tasha.

Nayeli:
From the Native American Zapotec, meaning "I love you."

Nelia:
From the Spanish meaning "yellow."

Nell:
See Eleanor, Elen, or Helen. *Alternative spelling:* Nelly.

Nelle:
Possibly from the Greek meaning "stone."

Nena:
See Nina.

Nereida:
From the Greek meaning "sea nymph" or "daughter of Nereus." *Alternative spellings:* Nereyda, Nerida, Nerissa, Neysa.

Nerissa:
See Nereida. *Alternative spelling:* Neysa.

Nerys:
From the Welsh possibly meaning "lordly."

Nevaeh:
A contemporary invented name. The word "heaven" spelled backward. *Alternative spelling:* Neveah.

Neveah
See Nevaeh.

Ngaio:
From the Maori meaning "clever."

Nia:
See Niamh.

Niamh:

From the Irish meaning "bright." *Short form:* Nia.

Nicole:

The feminine form of Nicholas (see Boys' Names). *Alternative spellings:* Niccole, Nichol, Nichola, Nichole, Nicholle, Nicholette, Nickole, Nicola, Nikkole, Nikole, Nycole. *Short forms:* Nicci, Nickey, Nicki, Nickie, Nicky, Nike, Niki, Nikia, Nikita, Nikkie, Nikki, Niquie.

Nicolette:

See Nicole. *Alternative spelling:* Nickolette.

Nigella:

The feminine form of Nigel (see Boys' Names).

Nike:

From the Greek meaning "victorious."

Niki:

See Nicole or Nikita.

Nikita:

From the Greek name *Aniketos*, meaning "unconquerable." *Short form:* Niki, Nikki.

Nina:

From the Spanish meaning "little girl", see also Antonia. *Alternative spellings:* Neena, Nena.

Ninon:

See Anne.

Niquie:

See Nicole.

Nirvana:

From the Hindi meaning "heaven" or "the extinguishing of a fire."

Nisha:

From the Hindi meaning "night."

Nissa:

From the Hebrew *nes,* meaning "sign" or "emblem."

Nita:

See Anita and Juanita.

Nitza:

From the Hebrew meaning "flower bud." *Alternative spelling:* Nitzana.

Noelle:

The feminine form of Noel (see Boys' Names). *Alternative spellings:* Noel, Noele, Noelia.

N

Noemi:
See Naomi.

Nola:
See Fenella.

Nona:
From the Latin meaning "nine."
Alternative spellings: Noni, Nonie.

Noor:
From the Arabic meaning "light."

Nora:
See Eleanor. *Alternative spelling:* Norah.

Noreen:
See Eleanor.

Norell:
From the Scandinavian meaning "from the north."

Noriko:
From the Japanese meaning "law" or "order."

Norma:
From the Latin meaning "pattern."

Nova:
From the Latin meaning "new."

Nuala:
See Fenella.

Nura:
From the Arabic meaning "light."

Nyasia:
From the Greek meaning "beginning."

Nyela:
From the Arabic name Najla, meaning "beautiful eyes."

Nyla:
From the Arabic meaning "winner."

Nyree:
From the Maori meaning "sea."

O

Oceana:
From the Greek meaning "ocean."

Octavia:
From the Latin meaning "eighth."
Alternative spellings: Octaviana,
Oktavia. *Short forms:* Tavi, Tavia, Tavie.

Odelia.
From the French meaning "wealthy"
or possibly the Hebrew meaning "I will
praise you." *Alternative spellings:* Odela,
Odella, Odette, Odila, Odile, Ottilie.

Odessa:
From the Greek meaning "wandering."

Olena:
See Helen.

Oletha:
From the Greek meaning "truth."

Olexa:
See Alexandra.

Olga:
A Russian form of Helga meaning
"prosperous" or "blessed." *Alternative
spellings:* Elga, Helga, Olenka. *Short
forms:* Oli, Ollie, Olly.

Olive:
See Olivia.

Olivia.
From the Latin *oliva,* meaning "olive."
Alternative spellings: Oliva, Olive,
Olivette. *Short forms:* Liv, Livia, Livvy,
Livy, Oli, Ollie, Olly.

Olwen:
From the Welsh meaning "white
footprint."

Olympia:
From the Greek meaning "from
Olympus." *Alternative spellings:*
Olympe, Olimpia, Olympie.

Ondine:
From the Latin meaning "wave."

Ondrea:
See Andrea.

Onora:
See Honor.

Oonagh:
From the Irish Gaelic meaning "lamb."
Alternative spellings: Una, Oona.

O

Opal:
From the Sanskrit meaning "jewel" or "gemstone."

Ophelia:
From the Greek meaning "to help."

Ophrah:
From the Hebrew meaning "young deer" or "place of dust." *Alternative spellings:* Ofra, Ofrah, Ophra, Oprah.

Ora:
From the Hebrew meaning "light."

Oralee:
From the Hebrew "the Lord is my light." *Alternative spellings:* Areli, Yareli.

Oralia:
The English form of Aurelia. *Alternative spelling:* Oralie.

Oriana:
From the Latin meaning "rising sun" or "morning sun." *Alternative spellings:* Oria, Oriande, Oriane, Orianne, Oriente.

Oriel:
From the Latin meaning "gold."

Oriola:
From the Latin meaning "golden bird."

Orla:
From the Gaelic Irish meaning "golden lady."

Ortensia:
From the Italian. A variant of Hortense.

Osma:
From the Old English meaning "divine protection."

Otilie:
From the Czech meaning "lucky heroine."

Oz:
From the Hebrew meaning "strength."

P

Padma:
From the Hindi meaning "lotus."

Pagan:
From the Old English meaning "country dweller."

Paige:
From the French meaning "young attendant" or the Old English meaning "child." *Alternative spellings:* Padge, Padget, Page.

Paisley:
From the Scottish place name.

Pallas:
From the Greek meaning "goddess."

Paloma:
From the Spanish meaning "dove." *Alternative spellings:* Palloma, Palomita, Peloma.

Pamela:
From the Greek meaning "honey." *Alternative spellings:* Pamala, Pammela. *Short forms:* Pam, Pammie, Pammy.

Pandora:
From the Greek meaning "highly gifted."

Pansy:
From the Greek meaning "flower" or "fragrant" or the French *penser,* meaning "to think."

Paola:
The Italian form of Paula.

Paris:
After the Greek mythological character. Also the capital city of France. *Alternative spelling:* Parris.

Parker:
From the English meaning "park keeper."

Parvati:
From the Sanskrit meaning "of the mountain."

Pascale:
From the French meaning "Easter" or the Hebrew *pesach,* meaning "pass over," relating to the festival of Passover. *Alternative spellings:* Paschal, Pasquale.

Patience:
From the Latin meaning "to suffer." *Short forms:* Pat, Pattie, Patty.

P

Patrice:
See Patricia.

Patricia:
From the Greek meaning "noble."
Alternative spellings: Patreece, Patrica,
Patrice, Patricka, Patrisha, Patrishia.
Short forms: Pat, Patsy, Pattie, Patty,
Tricia, Trisha.

Paula:
A feminine form of Paul (see Boys'
Names). *Alternative spellings:* Paola,
Paulene, Pauletta, Paulette, Pauli,
Paulie, Paulina, Pauline, Paullette, Pauly,
Pol, Polly.

Paulette:
See Paula.

Paulina:
See Paula.

Payton:
A feminine form of Patrick (see Boys'
Names). *Alternative spelling:* Peyton.

Pearl:
From the Latin meaning "jewel."

Pegeen:
See Margaret. *Alternative spelling:*
Peggeen.

Peggy:
See Margaret.

Pelagia:
From the Greek meaning "mermaid" or
"sea."

Penelope:
From the Greek meaning "weaver."
Short form: Penny.

Peninah:
From the Hebrew meaning "coral" or
"pearl." *Short forms:* Penina, Peninna.

Penny:
See Penelope.

Peony:
From the Greek meaning "praise giving"
or possibly from the flower.

Perdita:
From the Latin meaning "lost." *Short
forms:* Perdie, Perdy.

Peri:
From the Greek meaning "mountain
dweller" or the Persian meaning "fairy"
or "elf."

Perla:
The Spanish and Italian form of Pearl.

Perri:

From the Greek or Latin meaning "small rock" or "traveler"; the French meaning "pear tree"; or the Welsh meaning "daughter of Harry." *Alternative spellings:* Perrie, Perry.

Persephone:

From the Greek meaning "dazzling brilliance" or "she who destroys the light."

Peta:

See Petra.

Petra:

A feminine form of Peter (see Boys' Names). *Alternative spellings:* Peta, Petrea, Petrina, Pietra.

Petronella:

From the Greek meaning "small rock." *Alternative spellings:* Patronilla, Pernella, Petrona, Petronela, Petronelle.

Petula:

From the Latin meaning "seeker." *Alternative spelling:* Petulah.

Peyton:

See Payton.

Pheodora:

A feminine form of Theodore (see Boys' Names).

Philidelphia:

From the Greek meaning "brotherly love."

Phillippa:

The feminine form of Philip (see Boys' Names). *Alternative spellings:* Philipa, Phillipina, Phillippe, Phillippine. *Short forms:* Phil, Phillie, Philly, Pippa, Pippy.

Philomena:

Feminine form of the Latin name Philomenus, from the Greek *philein,* meaning "to love," and *menos,* meaning "strength." *Alternative spellings:* Filomena, Philomene, Philomina. *Short form:* Mena.

Phoebe:

From the Greek meaning "pure" or "bright." *Alternative spelling:* Phebe.

Phoenix:

From the Greek meaning "dark red." Also mythical bird that rose from the ashes.

Phylicia:

See Felicia. *Alternative spellings:* Philica, Philycia, Phylesia, Phylisha, Phyllecia.

Phyllis:

From the Greek meaning "foliage." *Alternative spellings:* Phillis, Philys, Phylis, Phyllys.

P

Pia:
From the Italian meaning "devout."

Pilar:
From the Latin meaning "pillar" or "column" or possibly from the Spanish *Nuestra Senora del Pilar,* meaning "Our Lady of the Pillar," a name for the Virgin Mary.

Piper:
From the English meaning "pipe player."

Pippa:
See Phillippa.

Pippi:
From the French meaning "rosy cheeked."

Placida:
From the Latin meaning "serene."

Polly:
See Paula or Mary.

Pomona:
From the Latin meaning "apple" or "fruit."

Poppy:
From the Latin meaning "poppy flower."

Porshe:
See Portia.

Portia:
From the Latin meaning "offering" or possibly from Latin porcus meaning "pig." *Alternative spellings:* Porche, Porsha, Porshe, Portiea.

Posey:
See Josephine.

Precious:
From the French meaning "precious" or "dear."

Presley:
From the English meaning "priest's meadow."

Primrose:
From the Latin meaning "first rose" or from the flower.

Princess:
From the English meaning "daughter of royalty."

Priscilla:
From the Latin meaning "primitive" or "ancient." *Alternative spellings:* Precilla, Pricilla, Priscella, Prisila, Prissilla. *Short forms:* Cilla, Piri, Pris, Prisca, Prissy.

Q–R

Queenie:
From the Old English meaning "Queen."
Alternative spelling: Queeny.

Quinn:
Possibly from the Old English word *cwen,*
meaning "Queen," or the Irish Gaelic
Caoin, meaning "counsel."

Quinta:
From the Latin meaning "fifth."

Rabiah:
From the Arabic meaning "fourth" or "fragrant
breeze." *Alternative spelling:*
Rabia.

Rachael:
From the Hebrew meaning "ewe,"
symbolizing innocence. *Alternative
spellings:* Rachel, Rachelle, Raquel,
Raquelle. *Short forms:* Rach, Rae, Ray.

Rachol:
See Rachael.

Radha:
From the Sanskrit meaning "success."

Rae:
See Rachael.

Raegan:
See Reagan.

Rafaela:
A feminine form of Raphael (see Boys'
Names).

Raina:
See Rayna

Rainbow:
From the Old English words *regn,* meaning
"rain," and *boga,* meaning "bow" or "arch."

Raine:
From the German meaning "mighty
army" or the French word *reine,* meaning
"Queen." *Alternative spelling:* Rayne,
Reine.

Raisa:
From the Russian meaning "paradise" or
the Yiddish meaning "rose." *Alternative
spelling:* Raissa.

R

Ramona:
A feminine version of Ramon (see Boys' Names).

Ranelle:
A feminine form of Rudolf or Randall (see Boys' Names).

Rani:
From the Hindi meaning "princess" or "queen."

Raquel:
See Rachael.

Rasa:
From the Lithuanian meaning "dew."

Raven:
From the English meaning "blackbird" or the French meaning "voracious." *Alternative spelling:* Ravenne.

Ravenne:
See Raven.

Ravette:
From the Old English meaning "sacred daughter."

Rayna:
From the Hebrew meaning "song of the Lord."

Reagan:
From the Irish meaning "little ruler." *Alternative spelling:* Raegan.

Reanna:
See Rhiannon.

Reba:
See Rebecca.

Rebecca:
From the Hebrew meaning "tied," implying "a faithful wife." *Alternative spellings:* Rebeca, Rebeka, Rebekah, Rivka, Rivkah. *Short forms:* Becca, Becky, Beka, Bekki, Bex, Reba, Riva.

Reese:
From the Welsh meaning "ardent" or "fiery." *Alternative spelling:* Reece.

Regan:
Possibly from the Irish *riogan,* meaning "queen," or from the Gaelic surname O'Riagáin. *Alternative spellings:* Reagan, Reagen.

Regina:
From the Latin meaning "queen." *Alternative spellings:* Reena, Reene, Regan, Reggie, Regine, Reina, Rena, Rene, Rina. *Short forms:* Gina, Geena.

Reina:
See Raine. *Alternative spelling:* Raina, Reyna.

Renata:
From the Latin meaning "born again."

René:
From the French meaning "reborn." *Alternative spellings:* Renee, Reenie.

Renée:
From the Latin *Renata*, meaning "reborn."

Rexanne:
See Roxanne.

Rhea:
From the Greek meaning "flowing stream" or "protectress."

Rhian:
See Rhiannon.

Rhiannon:
From the Welsh meaning "goddess" or "maiden." *Alternative spellings:* Reanna, Reanne, Rheanna, Rhian, Rhianna.

Rhoda:
From the Greek meaning "rose" or possibly "woman of Rhodes."

Rhona:
From the Scottish meaning "rough isle" or "fierce waters."

Ria:
See Maria.

Ricarda:
A feminine form of Richard (see Boys' Names). *Alternative spelling:* Richarda. *Short forms:* Ricky, Rikki.

Richelle:
A feminine form of Richard (see Boys' Names) or from the Old English *ric,* meaning "power."

Riley:
From the Gaelic Irish meaning "valiant."

Rilla:
From the Spanish meaning "little stream" or "little brook."

Rina:
A short form of Carina, Katarina, or Rionach or from the Hebrew meaning "joyful."

Riona:
From the Irish Gaelic name *rioghan,* meaning "queen."

R

Rionach:
From the Gaelic Irish meaning "queenly."

Risa:
From the Latin meaning "laughter."

Rita:
See Margaret.

Riva:
See Rebecca.

Roberta:
The feminine form of Robert (see Boys' Names). *Short forms:* Bobbette, Bobbi, Bobbie, Bobby, Bobbye, Bobina, Bobinette, Rebinah, Robbie, Robena, Robenia, Robin, Robina, Robine, Robinette, Robinia, Robyn, Rori, Rory, Ruby.

Robin:
See Roberta.

Rochelle:
From the Old German *hrok,* meaning "rest," or the French meaning "little rock"; see also Rachelle.

Roderica:
From the German meaning "famous ruler." *Short forms:* Rori, Rory.

Rohana:
From the Hindi and Sanskrit, meaning "sandalwood." *Alternative spelling:* Rohanna.

Róisín:
From the Irish meaning "rose."

Rolanda:
The feminine form of Roland (see Boys' Names).

Romola:
From the Latin, meaning "Roman woman."

Romy:
A short form of Rosemary.

Ronalda:
The feminine form of Ronald (see Boys' Names). *Short forms:* Rona, Roni, Ronna, Ronne, Ronnie.

Roni:
From the Hebrew meaning "song"; see also Ronalda.

Ronnie:
See Ronalda or Veronica.

Rosa:

From the Latin meaning "rose"; see also Rosamond or Rosalind. *Alternative spelling:* Rosalie.

Rosabel:

From the Latin words *rosa,* meaning "rose," and *belle,* meaning "beautiful." *Alternative spellings:* Rosabella, Rosabelle.

Rosaleen:

See Rosalind.

Rosalind:

From the Old German *hros* meaning "horse" and lind meaning "weak," "tender" or "soft." *Alternative spellings:* Rosaleen, Rosaline, Rosalyn, Rosalynn, Rosalynne, Roslyn. *Short forms:* Ros, Rosa, Rose, Roz.

Rosamond:

From the Latin meaning "rose of the world" or "rose of purity" or the German meaning "protector of the horse." *Alternative spelling:* Rosamund. *Short forms:* Ros, Rosa, Rose, Roz.

Rose:

From the Old German meaning "fame" or the flower; see also Rosalind, Rosamond. *Alternative spellings:* Rosie, Rosey.

Roseanne:

The combination of Rose and Anne.

Roselyn:

See Rosalind.

Rosemary:

From the Latin *ros marinus,* meaning "sea dew." *Alternative spelling:* Rosemarie. *Short forms:* Roma, Romy.

Rosetta:

From the Latin meaning "little rose."

Roshan:

From the Sanskrit meaning "shining light."

Rowan:

From the Irish Gaelic meaning "little red one"; possibly the Celtic meaning "clad in white" or from the tree. *Alternative spelling:* Rowen.

Rowena:

From the Celtic meaning "white spear" or the Welsh meaning "fair one" or "famous friend."

Roxanne:

From the Persian meaning "dawn." *Alternative spellings:* Rexanne, Rosana, Roxana, Roxane, Roxanna, Roxie, Roxine, Roxy.

R

R

Roya:
The feminine form of Roy (see Boys' Names).

Rubena:
From the Hebrew, meaning "see, a son." Feminine form of Reuben.

Ruby:
From the Latin word *rubinus,* meaning "red." *Alternative spelling:* Rubi.

Rumer:
From the English gypsies, possibly derived from "Romany."

Runa:
From the Norse meaning "to flow."

Ruta:
From the Lithuanian meaning "rue" (the herb).

Ruth:
From the Hebrew meaning "vision of beauty" or "companion." *Short forms:* Ruthi, Ruthie.

Ryan:
See Boys' Names. *Alternative spellings:* Rian, Rion, Ryana, Ryann, Ryen.

Ryesen:
From the English meaning "rye" or the Irish Gaelic name Róisín, meaning "rose."

Rylee:
From the Irish meaning Valiant. See also Riley.

Ryleigh:
See Rylee.

Rylie:
See Rylee.

S

Sabrina:
From the Latin meaning "the boundary mark" or the Hebrew meaning "thorny." *Alternative spellings:* Sabreena, Sabrena, Sabryna, Zabrina.

Sacha:
From the Greek meaning "help mate"; see also Alexandra. *Alternative spelling:* Sasha.

Sada:
From the Old English *saed*, meaning "seed," or the Hebrew meaning "support" or "help"; see also Sarah. *Alternative spellings:* Sadele, Sadelle, Sadie, Sady.

Sade:
From the Yoruban African meaning "honor confers a crown."

Sadie:
See Sarah.

Saffron:
From the Arabic meaning "crocus." *Short forms:* Saffie, Saffy.

Sage:
From the English meaning "wise one."

Sahara:
From the Arabic meaning "desert."

Saige:
A form of Sage.

Sal:
See Sarah.

Salena:
See Selina or Celine.

Salima:
From the Arabic meaning "unharmed."

Sally:
See Sarah.

Salma:
From the Arabic meaning "safe."

Samantha:
From the Aramaic meaning "listener." *Short forms:* Sam, Sami, Sammie, Sammy.

Samara:
From the Hebrew meaning "guarded by God." *Short forms:* Sam, Sami, Sammie, Sammy.

Samira:
From the Arabic meaning "to talk in the evening or night" or the Arabic meaning "pleasant" or "entertainer." *Short forms:* Sam, Sami, Sammi, Sammy.

 S

S

Sanaa:
From the Arabic meaning "mountaintop, splendid, brilliant."

Sancha:
From the Latin meaning "holy" or "pure." *Alternative spellings:* Cynthia, Sanchia.

Sandra:
See Alexandra. *Alternative spellings:* Sandrea, Saundra, Sondra, Zandra. *Short forms:* Sandee, Sandi, Sandy.

Sandrine:
From the French version of Alexandra.

Saniya:
From the Hindi meaning "pearl." *Alternative spelling:* Saniyah.

Santa:
From the Latin *sanctus,* meaning "holy." *Alternative spellings:* Santana, Santina.

Saoirse:
From the Irish Gaelic meaning "freedom."

Sapphire:
From the Arabic meaning "beautiful" or the Sanskrit meaning "beloved of Saturn." *Alternative spellings:* Safira, Sapphira.

Sara:
See Sarah.

Sarah:
From the Hebrew meaning "princess." *Alternative spellings:* Morag, Sada, Sadella, Sadie, Saira, Sairah, Sara, Sari, Sarina, Sarri, Sal, Sally, Shara, Shari, Sherrie, Sorcha, Zara, Zarah, Zaria, Zoreen, Zorna.

Sarahi:
See Sarah.

Sarai:
From the Hebrew meaning "princess."

Saraid:
From the Celtic meaning "excellent."

Sariah:
See Sarah.

Sasha:
See Sacha.

Saskia:
Possibly from the word *sachs,* meaning "Saxon."

Saturnia:
From the Latin *satus,* meaning "sowing" or "planting."

Savannah:
From the Spanish *zavana,* meaning "an expanse of open grassland." *Alternative spelling:* Savanna, Savonne.

Scarlet:
From the Old French referring to the color. *Alternative spelling:* Scarlett.

Sebastiane:
The feminine form of Sebastian (see Boys' Names). *Alternative spellings:* Sebastene, Sebastia, Sebastiana, Sebastienne.

Sela:
From the Hebrew meaning "rock." *Alternative spelling:* Selah.

Selima:
From the Arabic meaning "peaceful."

Selina:
From the Greek meaning "moon goddess." *Alternative spellings:* Celina, Salena, Selena, Selenia, Selene, Selenna, Selinda, Seline. *Short form:* Sena.

Selma:
From the Celtic meaning "fair" or the Norse meaning "divinely protected."

Sena:
See Selina.

Senga:
From the Scottish Gaelic *eang,* meaning "slender."

Seonaid:
See Janet.

September:
From the Latin *septum,* meaning "seven."

Septima:
From the Latin meaning "seventh."

Serafina:
From the Hebrew word *seraphim,* meaning "burning ones." *Alternative spellings:* Sarafina, Serafine, Seraphina, Seraphine, Serapia, Serofina.

S

Seren:

From the Welsh meaning "star."

Serena:

From the Latin *serenus,* meaning "calm" or "serene." *Alternative spellings:* Sirena, Sirenna, Syrena.

Serenity:

From the Latin *serenus,* meaning "calm" and "serene."

Sevina:

From the Latin *severus,* meaning "severe" or "stern."

Shaina:

From the Hebrew meaning "beautiful." *Alternative spelling:* Shayna.

Shakira:

From the Arabic meaning "thankful." *Alternative spelling:* Shaira.

Shalaidah:

From the Old Celtic meaning "wood nymph" or "from the fairy wood."

Shaley:

From the Old English *shelley,* meaning "clearing on or near a slope."

Shana:

From the Irish meaning "old" or "wise." *Alternative spellings:* Danna, Shan, Shanda, Shandi, Shane, Shannah.

Shania:

Possibly an English name derived from Shana or from the Native American meaning "on my way." *Alternative spelling:* Shaniyah.

Shannagh:

Possibly from the Irish Gaelic meaning "old" or "wise."

Shannon:

From the Irish Gaelic meaning "wise" or from the name of an Irish river.

Sharayah:

From the Hebrew meaning "friend."

Sharlene:

See Charlene.

Sharmilla:

From the Sanskrit meaning "happy."

Sharon:

From the Hebrew meaning "plain" or "flat area." *Alternative spellings:* Shareen, Sharron, Sharyn.

Shauna:
See Shona.

Shawna:
The feminine form of Shawn (see Boys' Names).

Shayla:
See Sheila.

Shaylee:
A form of Shea.

Shayna:
From the Hebrew meaning "beautiful" or "fine" or "goodly."

Shayne:
The feminine form of Shane (see Boys' Names).

Shea:
From the Irish meaning "courteous."

Sheba:
See Bathsheba.

Sheila:
From the Irish Gaelic *sile,* meaning "blind"; see also Celine. *Alternative spellings:* Shayla, Sheelagh, Sheelah, Shelagh, Shelia, Shelli, Shelly, Shielah.

Shelby:
From the English meaning "willow farm"; see also Shelley.

Shelda:
See Sheldon.

Sheldon:
Originally an English surname taken from the local areas in Derbyshire and Devon. *Short form:* Shelda.

Shelley:
From the English meaning "meadow on the ledge"; see also Michelle. *Alternative spellings:* Shelby, Shelli.

Sheree:
From the French *chérie,* meaning "dear" or "darling." *Alternative spellings:* Shereen, Sheri, Sherri, Sherrie, Sherry.

Shereen:
See Sheree.

Sheridan:
From the Gaelic Irish meaning "bright" or possibly "to seek."

Sherilyn:
A contemporary invented name. A blend of Sheryl and Marilyn.

S

Sherlyn:
A contemporary invented name. A blend of Sheryl and Lynn.

Sherry:
See Sheree.

Sheryl:
See Cheryl.

Shiloh:
From the Hebrew meaning "God's gift."

Shirley:
From the Old English *scir,* meaning "shire," and *leah,* meaning "meadow." *Alternative spellings:* Sheree, Sherill, Sherl, Sherri, Sherrie, Sherye, Sheryl, Shirl, Shirlee, Shirleen, Shirlene.

Shona:
A feminine form of Sean (see Boys' Names). *Alternative spellings:* Shaina, Shaine, Shana, Shanie, Shannon, Shauna, Shaune, Shonda, Shoni, Shonie.

Shoshana:
From the Hebrew meaning "lily." *Alternative spellings:* Shoshan, Shushan, Shushanah, Shoshanah, Siùsaidh, Sosanna, Sukey, Suki, Sukie, Susan, Susanna, Susanne, Suzanna, Suzanne, Suzette, Zsuzsana, Zuzana. *Short forms:* Su, Susan, Sue, Sukey, Susie, Susy, Suzey, Suzie, Suzy.

Shulamit:
From the Hebrew meaning "peacefulness." *Short form:* Shula.

Shyama:
From the Sanskrit meaning "dark."

Shyann:
See Cheyenne. *Alternative spelling:* Shyanne,

Shyla:
From the Hindi meaning "daughter of the mountain."

Sian:

See Jane. *Alternative spelling:* Siana.

Sibyl:

See Cybil. *Alternative spellings:* Sibil, Sibilla, Sibille, Sibley, Sibylla, Sibyllina, Sybella, Sybil, Sybille, Sybyl, Sybylla.

Sidney:

See Boys' Names. *Alternative spellings:* Cydney, Sidoney, Sidonie, Sidonia, Sydney. *Short form:* Sid, Syd.

Sidonie:

See Sidney. *Alternative spelling:* Sidonia.

Sidra:

From the Latin meaning "star."

Siegfrieda:

The feminine form of Siegfried (see Boys' Names).

Sienna:

From the Italian city.

Sierra:

From the Spanish meaning "beautiful mountains."

Sigmunda:

From the German meaning "victorious protector."

Signa:

From the Latin meaning "signal."

Sigrid:

From the Scandinavian meaning "beautiful" or "victorious"; see also Siegfrieda. *Short form:* Siri.

Silvana:

See Silvia.

Silvia:

From the Latin *silva,* meaning "wood." *Alternative spellings:* Silvana, Silvano, Silvannam, Silvina, Sylverta, Sylvi, Sylvia, Sylvie, Sylvina, Sylvonna, Zilvia.

Simone:

From the French meaning "hear" or "listen" or the feminine form of Simon (see Boys' Names). *Alternative spellings:* Simona, Simonne, Symone.

Sincád:

A Gaelic Irish form of Jane.

Siobhán:

A Gaelic form of Jane.

Sirena:

From the Greek *seiren,* meaning "to bind" or "to attack"; see also Serena.

S

Siri:
From the Scandinavian goddess of humor; see also Sigrid.

Sirios:
From the Greek meaning "glowing" or "burning."

Sisley:
See Cecilia.

Skye:
From the Scottish Island.

Skyla:
From the Dutch meaning "scholar" or possibly "sheltering." *Alternative spellings:* Skylar, Skyler. *Short forms:* Sky, Skye.

Slaney:
From the Irish Gaelic meaning "challenge."

Sloane:
From the Scottish Gaelic meaning "fighter" or "warrior." *Alternative spelling:* Sloan.

Sofia:
See Sonya. *Alternative spellings:* Sofiah, Sofie, Sophie.

Soma:
From the Sanskrit meaning "moon" or the Greek meaning "body."

Sona:
From the Latin meaning "to make a noise" or "to cry out."

Sonia:
See Sonya.

Sonya:
From the Greek *sofya,* meaning "wisdom." *Alternative spellings:* Sofia, Sofie, Sonia, Sonja, Sonya, Sophia, Sophie.

Sophia:
See Sonya.

Sophie:
See Sonya.

Soraya:
From the Persian meaning "princess."

Sorcha:
From the Gaelic meaning "bright"; see also Sarah.

Sorrel:
From the plant of the same name or the Old French meaning "sour."

Sri:
From the Sanskrit meaning "light" or "beauty."

Stacey:
Possibly from Anastasia or the Greek meaning "rich in corn"; also the feminine form of Eustace (see Boys' Names). *Alternative spellings:* Stace, Staci, Stacie, Stacy, Statsia.

Star:
From the Latin *stella,* meaning "star."

Stella:
From the Latin meaning "star"; see also Estelle.

Stephanie:
The feminine form of Stephen (see Boys' Names). *Alternative spellings:* Stefana, Stefani, Stefania, Stefanie, Steffanie, Steffany, Steffi, Stephani, Stephania, Stephany, Stephine, Stevie.

Suki:
From the Japanese meaning "beloved."

Summer:
From the Old English *sumor,* meaning "summer." *Alternative spelling:* Somer.

Sunita:
From the Sanskrit meaning "well-behaved."

Sunni:
From the Scandinavian name Sunniva meaning "gift of the sun." See also Sunny.

Sunny:
From the Old English *sunne,* meaning "bright" or "sunny" or "cheerful." *Alternative spelling:* Sunni.

Susan:
From the Hebrew meaning "lily." *Short form:* Susie, Sukey, Suzy.

Susana:
A form of Susan. *Alternative spellings:* Susanna, Susannah, Suzanne, Suzette. *Short form:* Sanna.

Sybil:
See Cybil.

Sydney:
Feminine form of Sidney. (see Boys' Names). *Alternative spelling:* Sydnee.

Sylvia:
See Silvia.

Tabitha:

From the Aramaic meaning "gazelle." *Alternative spelling:* Tabatha. *Short forms:* Tab, Tabbie, Tabby.

Talia:

From the Hebrew meaning "dew from heaven." *Alternative spelling:* Taliyah.

Tamara:

From the Arabic meaning "palm tree" or "seed of the palm tree." *Short forms:* Tam, Tami, Tammie, Tammy, Tamy.

Tamarind:

From the Arabic *tamr hindi,* meaning "Indian date palm." *Short forms:* Tam, Tami, Tammie, Tammy, Tamy.

Tamia:

A contemporary invented name. A blend of Tammy and Tania.

Tamsin:

A feminine form of Thomas (see Boys' Names). *Alternative spellings:* Tamsyn, Tamzen, Tamzin. *Short forms:* Tam, Tami, Tammie, Tammy, Tamy.

Tania:

From the Russian meaning "fairy queen"; see also Tatiana. *Alternative spellings:* Taniya, Taniyah, Tanya.

Tara:

From the Irish Gaelic meaning "hill."

Tarina:

From the Hebrew meaning "legend" or "story."

Taryn:

A contemporary invented name. A form of Tara.

Tasha:

From the Russian meaning "independent"; see also Natasha.

Tate:

From the Scandinavian meaning "cheerful."

Tatiana:

From the Russian after the King Tatius of the Sabines. *Alternative spelling:* Tatyana. *Short form:* Tania.

Tatum:

From the Middle English *tayt,* meaning "cheerful," "spirited."

Tatyana:

See Tatiana.

Tawny:

From the Irish meaning "a green field."

Taya:

Possibly from the Italian or Latin meaning "unknown." *Alternative spelling:* Tèa.

Taylor:

From the Middle English meaning "tailor, to cut."

Teagan:

From the Irish meaning "little poet." *Alternative spelling:* Teagen, Tegan.

Tegwen:

From the Welsh meaning "beautiful," "fair," or "pretty."

Teresa:

From the Greek meaning "harvest." *Alternative spellings:* Theresa, Thérèse. *Short form:* Tess, Tessa, Terri, Terry.

Terry:

A short form of Teresa. *Alternative spellings:* Teri, Terri.

Tess:

See Teresa.

Tessa:

See Teresa.

Thalia:

From the Greek *thallein,* meaning "to flourish."

Thea:

See Dorothea.

Thelma:

From the Greek meaning "wish" or "will."

Theodora:

From the Greek meaning "gift of God."

Thora:

From the Norse meaning "the thunderer."

Tia:

A short form of Cynthia or Letitia.

Tiana:

Possibly from the Greek meaning "princess" or a familiar form of Tatiana. *Alternative spelling:* Tianna.

Tiara:

From the Latin meaning "crowned."

Tiffany:

From the Greek meaning "manifestation of God."

T–U

Tina:
See Christina.

Toni:
See Antonia.

Topaz:
Named after the gemstone.

Tori:
From the Japanese meaning "bird." Also a familiar form of Victoria.

Tracy:
From the Latin *tractare,* meaning "to manage," "handle," "lead," "follow," or "investigate." *Alternative spellings:* Tracey, Traci. *Short form:* Trace.

Tricia:
See Patricia. *Alternative spelling:* Trisha.

Trina:
See Katrina.

Trinity:
From the Latin meaning "Triad."

Trixie:
See Beatrix.

Trudy:
From the German meaning "strength."

Tyler:
From the English meaning "a worker in roof tiles."

Tyra:
From the Scandinavian meaning "battler."

Ula:
From the Old English meaning "owl"; the Irish meaning "sea jewel"; or the Old German meaning "inheritor"; (see also Ursula).

Ulla:
From the German or Swedish meaning "willful."

Ulrica:
From the German meaning "wolf ruler" or "ruler of all." Alternative spellings: Ulrika, Ulrike, Ullrica, Ullrika. Short forms: Uli, Ully.

Uma:
From the Hindi meaning "mother."

Ursula:
From the Latin meaning "little she-bear." Alternative spellings: Ursala, Ursela, Ursella, Ursilla, Ursola. Short forms: Ula, Ursa.

V

Valentina:
From the Latin *valens,* meaning "strong" and "healthy." Alternative spellings: Valentin, Valentine.

Valeria:
See Valerie.

Valerie:
From the Latin *valere,* meaning "to be strong" or "to be healthy." Alternative spellings: Valeria, Valery, Valora.

Vanessa:
Created by the *Gulliver's Travels* author Jonathan Swift for his friend Esther Vanhomrigh by taking the first syllable of her surname and Essa, a pet form of Esther. Alternative spelling: Venessa. Short forms: Ness, Nessa, Nessie.

Vashti:
From the Persian meaning "beautiful."

Vedrana:
From the Yugoslavian *vedra,* meaning "bright" or "happy."

Venetia:
Possibly from the Latin meaning "of Venice" or the Latin word *venia,* meaning "kindness," "mercy," "forgiveness."

Vera:
From the Latin meaning "true" or the Russian meaning "faith."

Verena:
From the Latin meaning "truthful."

Verity:
From the Latin meaning "truth" or "truthful."

Veronica:
From the Latin *vera icon,* meaning "true image." Alternative spellings: Véronic, Veronika, Véronique. Short forms: Roni, Ronnie, Ronny, Veron.

Victoria:
From the Latin meaning "victory." Alternative spellings: Victoire, Victoriana, Victorie, Victorina, Viktoria, Vitoria, Vittoria. Short forms: Vicki, Vickie, Vicks, Vicky, Viki, Vikki, Vix.

Viola:
From the Latin word *violetta,* meaning "violet."

Violet:
From the Latin meaning "purple." One of the earliest flower names, first used in the 1830s.

V–W

Virginia:
From the Latin *virginitas,* meaning "pure," or possibly from the Latin *virginius,* meaning "manly race." Short forms: Ginnie, Ginny, Ginger, Jinny.

Vita:
From the Latin meaning "life."

Vivian:
From the Latin meaning "living," "alive." Alternative spellings: Vivien, Vivienne.

Viviana:
See Vivian.

Wenda:
From the Gaelic meaning "fair" or the Old Norse meaning "to change course," "to move forward," "to travel."

Wendy:
Created by J.M. Barrie in *Peter Pan*.

Whitley:
From the Middle English meaning "white meadow."

Whitney:
From the Middle English meaning "by the white island."

Wilfrida:
The feminine form of Wilfred (see Boys' Names).

Wilhelmina:
A feminine form of William (see Boys' Names). Alternative spellings: Wilhelma, Willetta, Wilmena. Short forms: Bill, Billie, Billy, Minnie, Willa, Willi, Willy, Wilma.

Willow:
From the slender and graceful wood tree.

Wilma:
See Wilhelmina.

Winifred:
From the Welsh meaning "blessed reconciliation" or the Old English meaning "friend of peace." Alternative spellings: Winefred, Winfred. Short forms: Fred, Freda, Freddi, Freddie, Fredi, Win, Winnie, Winny, Wyn.

Winona:
From the Native American Sioux meaning "first-born daughter." Alternative spelling: Wynona.

X–Y

Xanthe:
From the Greek meaning "yellow haired." Alternative spellings: Xantha, Zanthe.

Xenia:
From the Greek meaning "hospitality." Alternative spelling: Zenia.

Ximena:
An Old Spanish or Basque feminine form of Simon (see Boys' Names).

Xiomara:
From the Aramaic meaning "joyful deer."

Yadira:
From the Hebrew meaning "friend."

Yamilet:
A form of Jamilah.

Yareli:
A form of Oralee.

Yaretzi:
From the Aztec meaning "you will always be loved."

Yaritza:
A contemporary invented name. A blend of Yana and Ritsa.

Yasmine:
From the Arabic meaning "jasmine flower." Alternative spellings: Yasmeen, Yasmin, Yasmina, Yasmine.

Yelena:
See Helen.

Yesenia:
From the Arabic meaning "flower."

Yolande:
From the Greek meaning "violet" or the Latin meaning "modest." Alternative spelling: Yolanda.

Yoselin:
See Jocelyn.

Ysabel:
See Isabelle.

Yuliana:
See Juliana.

Yuridia:
Possibly from the Greek meaning "noblewoman."

Yvonne:
From the French meaning "yew." Alternative spellings: Ivette, Yvette.

Z

Zabrina:
See Sabrina.

Zahrah:
From the Arabic meaning "flower blossom." Alternative spellings: Zahara, Zaharah, Zahra.

Zaina:
From the Arabic meaning "beautiful."

Zandra:
See Sandra.

Zanthe:
See Xanthe.

Zara:
From the Arabic meaning "splendor" or from Arabic *zahr,* meaning "flower"; see also Sarah. *Alternative spelling:* Zarah.

Zaria:
From the Arabic word *zahr,* meaning "flower." *Alternative spelling:* Zariah.

Zelda:
Possibly from the Yiddish name Zelde meaning "happiness and good fortune" or a shortened form of Griselda.

Zenia:
See Xenia.

Zenobia:
From the Greek *zen,* meaning "gift," and *bios,* meaning "life." Alternative spellings: Xenobia.

Zeta:
Uncertain meaning, possibly from the English meaning "rose."

Zhane:
Possibly from the Arabic meaning "to shine." Alternative spellings: Shane.

Zillah:
From the Hebrew meaning "shade." Alternative spellings: Zilla, Zita.

Zinah:
From the Arabic meaning "adornment." Alternative spellings: Zina.

Zion:
From the Hebrew meaning "highest point."

Zita:
From the Italian meaning "a girl"; the Greek *zetein,* meaning "to seek"; or the Spanish meaning "rose."

Zoe:
From the Greek meaning "life." Alternative spellings: Zoey, Zoie, Zola.